THE
WOMEN WRITERS'
HANDBOOK

Edited by;
Robson, Georgeson, Beck.

With thanks to Yvon Grace.

AURORA METRO PUBLICATIONS

This edition published 1990

British Library Cataloguing in Publication Data.

THE WOMEN WRITERS' HANDBOOK
1. Great Britain. Publishing industries
I ROBSON, Cheryl, II GEORGESON, Vania, BECK, Janet.
338.4707050941

ISBN 0- 951-5877- 0 - 6

Typeset by Unicorn Publishing Studio
63, Jeddo Road, London W12 9EE

PRINTED AND BOUND BY POLPRINT
63 Jeddo Road, London W12 9EE. Tel: 081-749 0777

THE WOMEN WRITERS' HANDBOOK

Janet Beck taught Drama for two years in Brent, worked in Theatre in Education, and at Hull Rape Crisis Centre. Her first play, MY MICHELLE, was developed through the Soho Poly's Blueprints scheme for young writers, and she is currently collaborating on a second play. She teaches video and drama projects with young people, and works part-time at Willesden Green Library Centre, and with The Women Writers' Workshop.

Vania Georgeson worked as a Drama teacher in Brent for two years and then went on to devise and write a community play in conjunction with The Fleet Community Education Centre. She works as a freelance drama specialist in schools and colleges and has seen her work performed during the Attic Work Season. She is continuing to develop her work through the workshops and is currently the Literary Manager of The Women Writers' Workshops.

Cheryl Robson studied Drama and French at Bristol University then worked in film editing and production at the B.B.C. for several years, before freelancing. She has lectured in Higher Education and is currently taking her M.A. in Playwriting at Birmingham University. She was the Literary Manager for Bristol Express Theatre Company from 1988 — '90 and has written several plays. O ARCHITECT! was seen at the New End in Hampstead in 1989.

CONTENTS

CONTACTS

compiled by Jean Abbott.

BIBLIOGRAPHY

INTRODUCTION

The group at The Drill Hall Arts Centre in London, began in September 1986. Cheryl Robson was training as a drama teacher at the time and wanted to use drama skills as part of a writers' workshop for women. Having been a member herself of two mixed writers workshops for three years, she decided an all-women workshop was needed.

Bryony Lavery, an experienced writer and workshop leader offered practical advice, mentioning a book that she'd found useful, Viola Spolin's *Improvisation for the Theatre*. Cheryl faced the first fifteen members with some apprehension. The first year was difficult and isolated as she felt her way towards structuring workshops to help specifically in the development of the varied writing that the group produced. But it was worthwhile, because by the summer there were several promising pieces of work; plays, poems and short stories which were read and performed in the Drill Hall Theatre in May 1987, under the direction of Carole Pluckrose. It was time to move forward.

Whilst training as a drama teacher at Middlesex Polytechnic, Cheryl had met and worked with Janet Beck, who now joined Cheryl in devising and leading the fortnightly workshops. At weekly meetings new ideas for developing the workshop were discussed. One of the first of these, was the idea to introduce monthly Script Development Sessions, where work in progress was developed through first draft to performance in *Attic Work*.

This was to become an annual event, showcasing the new work to the public and an audience of theatre professionals. *Attic Work '88* was co-directed by Heather Goodman of Temba Theatre Company and Catherine Carnie of The Park Theatre and was supported practically by The Drill Hall Arts Centre, who gave us the use of the theatre, and helped with advertising and publicity, and financially by Greater London Arts. Of the dozen or so women who had their work performed, four were approached and had their work taken up by a literary agent, a television producer and a women's theatre company.

9

Two years on, the workshop had a core of members who had been attending regularly alongside new members who joined each term. This meant the workshop was operating on two levels: some members had work that had been developed and completed, others were beginners who needed encouragement to start writing. In September 1989, we divided the workshop into a Beginners' Group and a Second Stage Writers' Group, with Ayshe Raif joining as a guest tutor for the Spring term in 1990. *Attic Work '89* took the form of a 6 week research and development season of new work — playreadings, an anthology show and a Forum on Women's Writing called *The Way Forward*. Women attended from writers' workshops around the country and took part in a discussion which produced the idea of organising an International Festival of Women's Theatre for 1992.

As the last major festival of Women's Theatre had taken place in 1982, it was felt that it was high time to celebrate women's work in the theatre again and to seek an even more high-profile arena to do this in. A fair amount of controversy arose between those who thought the best of women's theatre should be promoted and staged at places like The National Theatre and those who argued for open access and a high degree of community theatre involvement in the Festival.

Invited speakers provided advice and information on writing for theatre, publishing, radio and television. They were Kate Harwood, Literary Manager of the Royal Court Theatre, Carole Spedding, Publishing Consultant and Organiser of Feminist Book Fortnight, Caroline Raphael, Editor of Drama on Radio 4, Ruth Baumgarten, Script Editor B.B.C. Television Drama, Susan Croft, founder of The New Playwright's Trust and Ayshe Raif, Writer for stage, screen and radio. The idea of an International Festival of Women's Theatre was taken up and a steering group was formed subsequently to explore the possibility of this. Research is currently underway to explore ways of funding the festival and the kind of organisational structure that would be most effective.

Contacts were also made with other women working in theatre and a joint programme of new work was developed with The Women's Theatre Group for 1990. Collaboration with an experienced producing company seems to offer a good deal of potential for successfuly realising new dramatic plays.

A number of members of the group were invited to read their own poetry at a meeting of the Sappho Lesbian Writers' Group and this exchange took place in March 1990. For writers of short stories and poetry, publication is often the best course of action.

The Workshop has set up links with publishers such as Sheba and The Women's Press. This book, published with the help of Carole Spedding and financial assistance from Greater London Arts, offers these members of the workshop the chance to see their work in print. We hope it will help other women writers initiate their own workshops and festivals of new writing throughout the country.

SETTING UP A WORKSHOP

In considering the kind of workshop you wish to set up, an awareness of the ways in which different groups function can be useful. There are three kinds of workshop:
1. Releasing Creativity sessions.
2. The therapy/support group.
3. Development of craft skills.

Releasing Creativity sessions are based on the premise that anyone can write and are aimed at being accessible to the community or specific sections of it. Although some members may go on to write seriously, they are more concerned with enabling people to recognise, use and enjoy their creativity.

The development of craft skills is often pitched at a more professional level with sessions looking at specific techniques or topics such as structure, dialogue, sub-text etc. Led by a writer/teacher they may hinder the development of the writer's voice by the concentration on perfecting techniques and styles copied from other 'classic' writers. This group of workshops comprises director-led projects formed to undertake a specific task such as writing a community play, or the kind of projects run by local libraries to publish a book of a group's writings.

Workshops can become mutual support groups. Whilst we reject the idea that writing workshops should not address the needs of individuals within the group, 'support groups' can be more useful in serving the needs of the writers than the needs of their scripts.

The Women Writers' Workshop currently runs two writing classes: *The Beginners' Class* integrates all three aspects mentioned above. It starts from the position that each member has a unique voice both as a woman and a writer and that members have different needs and priorities to more experienced writers. These may well include the exploration of personal, psychological or emotional issues through writing.

These writing workshops operate at an emotional level to inspire writers, as well as at an intellectual, technical level, in order to teach craft skills. Women in this group often start writing on an autobiographical basis and the group needs to feel safe and supportive enough for them to develop and share their work and experiences.

The leader seeks to focus and direct these explorations in order to facilitate the development of new skills and projects. Whilst allowing the woman space to explore her own needs, the emphasis should be on the writing itself. The beginners' class includes sessions on specific writing techniques, as well as sessions on themes suggested by the group and includes a writing and evaluation task as part of every session.

Second Stage the group for experienced writers, focusses on the development of professional craft skills and on individual members' work-in-progress. Sessions comprise both input from a leader and discussion/development of members' projects.

Professionals are invited to lead sessions on specific areas such as Caroline Raphael's workshop on writing Radio Drama and Susan Dunnett's talk on the work of a Literary Agent.

Members provide information on competitions and requests for new scripts and the group operates on a more cohesive basis. Members may choose to lead a session of their own devising to explore an idea. Resources and experiences are shared for the benefit of the group. Commitment is high and members are expected to produce new work with regularity.

Both workshops seek to produce new work for Script Development sessions and rehearsed readings, which serve individual writers by concentrating on a single script. By using the skills of a director and actors to improvise around themes and ideas problem areas may be identified and new material generated.

We believe that a writer should have a first draft of a script before undertaking one of these sessions or else the process can become one of group devising, instead of serving the writer's unique concept and ideas. It was found to be essential that a director had time to read a script in advance and discuss ideas for exercises and improvisations with the writer before the session.

The writer needs to be given permission to stop or 'freeze' the action at any stage if they feel that an improvisation is going in the wrong direction. A relationship with a director that has been established beforehand can go a long way to avoiding misunderstandings during the session.

If rehearsed readings or workshop productions become a substitute for full production of a dramatic play, writers may become discouraged and it is important for writers' workshops to establish links with directors and producing companies so that a piece of theatre can finally be tested before a public audience.

Defining The Group.

The Women Writers' Workshop has no selection criteria for membership and is open to any woman who has the desire to write. We have an Equal Opportunities policy and aim to be as accessible as possible. However, whilst there are obvious points to consider in setting up the group e.g. disabled access, there are other, hidden, or unacknowledged pressures which may prevent women from attending. These may arise from the choice of:

1) Venue.

Most of our members heard about the original group via the Drill Hall Arts Centre's publicity and mailing list. This has made the group particularly accessible to lesbian feminists. The Drill Hall does not have disabled access to the upper floors and so disabled beginners are disadvantaged. The Second Stage class is fully accessible, but the Bloomsbury does not have the same drop-in atmosphere as the Drill Hall, with the bar opening only when there is a show in the theatre main house.

Some venues are 'Arts Centres' in the sense of large, central theatre venues with bar/cafe facilities, offering many other events/workshops simultaneously. Arts Centres usually have a mailing/membership list and publicity budget for workshops. They may also offer help with administration and photocopying. But, they may alienate women who do not have a tradition of visiting them.

'Community Arts Centres' place their main emphasis on access for the local community and tend to be in a strong, local network. They have links with community life and offer creche facilities etc. They may offer help with administration and good, local publicity. They often house other events and classes, usually in the daytimes and there is the possibility of joining with other groups for readings of work/shows.

Other options are Women's Centres which can offer a 'women-only' space, Adult Education Institutes, Theatres or Schools. But each have their own set of expectations and will attract different women. In Adult Education, for example, women may expect to

15

be 'taught' rather than take part in experiential learning using drama skills issues of race and class must be addressed.

2) Time.

In general, evening classes are more accessible to working women, daytime classes to women with school-age children, unemployed women, or women who may fear travelling alone at night. The nature of the location and the provision of street lighting will also affect the attendance of women to evening classes. Cheap or free Creche facilities will help women attend who cannot afford the cost of childcare, but facilities are often only available during the day.

Transport is an important consideration when deciding on class times. Rural areas may not be served by public transport at certain times and metropolitan areas will be affected by the rush-hour. You may wish to build in time for socialising/visiting the theatre etc. but may had to be aware of the needs of single women travelling home at night.

3) Fee.

If you wish to make real concessions to unwaged/low-waged women, you will be forced to seek outside funding. You can apply to your local Education Authority for the group to become part of the Adult Education programme. Rates charged are set by the Authority, which collects membership fees from the class. Tutors are paid an hourly fee and employed by the Authority.

Classes which do not take place on the Authority's premises, are regarded as off-site classes. Funds are not usually available to cover room-hire, photocopying, publicity, postage or telephone costs that the tutor may incur. Adult Education Institutes include details of their classes in the termly prospectus.

Many writing workshops are attached to theatres or theatre companies and they are resourced by money from the theatre subsidy which is allocated to developing new writing. Some companies apply for separate funding specifically to finance workshops, but there is little continuity if the funding cannot be guaranteed from one term to the next. Where money is available to fund these workshops, writers are often invited to attend, sometimes with the additional request that they pay an administration fee.

Before accepting funding, consider how this might affect the nature of the group, the content or style of the class and the way in which members are selected.

If you fund the workshop informally, by charging what you need to cover room-hire, dependent on the number of women in the group, then you may want to decide on an appropriate fee for yourself to cover postage, telephone, travel expenses and administration, even if you do not pay yourself for your time.

Creating Boundaries

It often helps to work out certain limits for the group beforehand, in order to make the group a safe place for women to share their work and ideas.

Around a dozen women seems to be the right number for a group to work well together. Too few members, and the group will feel uncomfortably small for leader and members. Too many, and women will not get the time and attention they need.

We have tried to balance the length of the session with the number of members in the group, and have found that two hour sessions are good for smaller groups, three hours for larger or beginners' groups. When considering a longer session, a timed break can avoid the necessity of women leaving the room, and reinforce a safe structure, which you can also help to create by starting and finishing on time.

A break can be used as part of the structure. We usually break after the writing task, but before reading and discussing work. This is because, in many ways, our sessions have split into two distinct activities, not always of equal length. The first part is very much a personal process, with discussion, group and individual exploration of a theme or experience. The second part is more analytical, with the reading and sharing of work, offering opinions, and analysing achievements and problems within the writing.

These two demand different skills and a break can provide a transition between them. There is also a feeling of relief and a lessening of tension, associated with finishing writing and women may need to have a drink and a chat, or a change of scene before sharing their work with others.

We have also tended to meet fortnightly rather than weekly and we have found this beneficial for leader and group alike. Constant preparation of new material in response to group demands takes time and energy and the group may take time to assimilate it between meetings.

17

It is perhaps useful in setting boundaries, to meet in a public building rather than a private home. This can give the group a distinct beginning and end time and avoids imposing on one member. It also provides a regular space that the group can identify with.

Will it be a course that runs for a specified time, such as ten weeks? Will it be an ongoing workshop with members joining at any time, or a group taking new members only once a term or once a year? These are choices you should make before you start, so that members are clear at the outset.

By June 1989, three years after the Women Writers' Workshop had first started, six women had been attending throughout that period, whereas most women simply attended for the course of a year. Among these six members, an atmosphere of trust and a knowledge and appreciation of each others' work and process had been long established. They were operating as a sub-group and felt ill-disposed to new members altering the group's internal dynamics. For new members it was difficult and intimidating to come up against this sub-group, and for us, as leaders it was difficult to cater for the different needs of new and long- standing members in the same group.

They wanted and neeeded a different kind of structure to develop their work further. By now, they had all seen their work presented publicly and were engaged in the redrafting of long-term projects. Some had been commissioned, published and produced. With a high level of commitment and group cohesion, they needed to spend more time discussing and developing their work-in-progress, instead of constantly generating new material and ideas.

These six women became the core of the Second Stage class which began in September 1989.

How to set up your own Workshop

If you'd like to set up your own workshop there are a number of things to consider.
1. Discuss with another writer what the aims of the group would be and whether it would be specific to one genre of writing, e.g. poetry or playwriting.
2. Discuss whether it will be for women, and run by women and whether male agents, producers, publishers, directors, actors will

be invited to the group, or excluded from it.

3. Discuss whether the group will be for beginners only, for a wider spectrum of experience, or for experienced writers only.

4. Discuss if you want one leader or whether the workshop will be led each week by a different member of the group.

5. Find a venue for holding workshops. If you start off meeting in your own home, be aware that commitment may be lacking from other members. If you can find a cheap space to rent, share the cost of room hire by charging each member a small fee.

6. Advertise your workshop in newspapers, libraries, women's centres, nurseries, supermarkets and newsletters. Follow-up any inquiries with a typed sheet of information about the group and times of meetings. If possible talk to new members beforehand, if only by telephone.

7. Contact your local community resource centre and ask for access to cheap photocopying, printing etc. Members of the group should be encouraged to provide enough scripts for each character in the play. If the writer can sit and listen to the script rather being involved in reading it, she is likely to understand more about any problems that are inherent.

8. Contact your local women's centre, theatre, youth centre or Adult Education Institute for financial support to pay tutors and room hire and to cover the costs for photocopying, telephone and postage. You might wish to make an application for funding to an Arts Funding Body.

9. Always look out for new ideas to bring to the workshop and invite guest speakers or workshop leaders for one-off sessions to ensure that the sessions don't get stale and tired. A group from a wide variety of social backgrounds will help to make it lively and a sensitive leader with the ability to listen carefully and respond thoughtfully can make all the difference.

10. Make contact with other similar workshops and organise joint events/publications/readings.

WORKSHOP PROCESS

In using the following exercises, it's important that each stage is negotiated with members of the group so that needs and feelings which may arise are given time to be addressed. For this reason we leave it up to workshop leaders to decide how much time to allow for each stage, but the examples given were generally devised to fill a three hour session. Sometimes, what came up during the session meant that work was carried over to the following week. An awareness of the dynamics of an all–women group can go a long way towards helping create the right kind of working relationship between group members and between members and the workshop leader.

By sharing the ways in which we approach writing, an important understanding of the process of writing can be developed. Some of the stages we go through can be examined. Some writers go through a linear process of immersion in new material, absorption of that material, and then finally the transformation of that material into written form. Others piece their work together in a much more fragmentary way, as though creating a jig–saw puzzle which will only be completed when they have the final piece. There are those who believe that writing is almost a religious experience which can only take place when the writer is in the right mood, wildly inspired, or lucky enough to be visited at night by their Muse. Others approach writing as the study of a very specific craft which they will be able to improve by the development and practice of technical skills.

Whatever the process a writer develops to get to the point of writing, and to continue writing, support and encouragement of this conceptual and experimental stage of the work will enable the final product to be realised successfully.

Many women who come to the workshops have never attended a women only group before and as they work together, they participate in a process of valuing each other's writing. By taking each other's ideas and writing seriously, an attitude of mutual trust and respect is achieved. In this way, women can share and explore personal, often very intimate experiences in a supportive and caring atmosphere. Initial embarrassment and the urge to compete with other women for the attention of the workshop leader, can be accommodated if the workshop leader is able to acknowledge the individual needs of different members and to provide the encouragement many women need who have difficulties in expressing themselves.

A group comprising women of different age, race, class and sexuality offers a rich variety of experience and perspectives. In respecting and positively welcoming diverse opinions, the workshop leader ensures that value is not attached to one dominant perspective. Materials can be examined for their intrinsic values and attempts made to provide examples of writing from a wide range of cultural experience.

However, searching for "common ground" and an exploration of differing attitudes to shared experience cannot always resolve a conflict between the distinct needs of group members, and can occasionally be counter–productive, if a conflict is not addressed. It can escalate and lead to members leaving the group. Conflicts may arise, for example, between specifically feminist women, attending a women's group for political reasons, and women who may be alienated by such views. In some cases, it may be necessary to make a choice, and this involves prioritising who the class is for: it may be that the class is based in a strong, local community and the leader feels it should primarily serve the community's needs.

Groups often follow a pattern in the course of establishing themselves. Be prepared for the group to change week by week, and it may even show signs of disintegration around the middle of the process. Generally, a group will go through the following stages:
1. The workshop leader offers a lot of support to members who show dependency and fear of rejection.
2. Members worry about the expectations of the group and the leader and fear exposing themselves too much.
3. Arguments arise between members, who enact feelings of rivalry and repeat patterns of previous female relationships such as their mother/daughter relationship.
4. Members form sub–groups to provide identity for themselves by connection with others. Co–operation and mutual trust become a feature.

5. A cohesive group finally emerges, focussed and fully committed to the work of the group.

If members depart and join rival groups, it can leave others with feelings of abandonment. Some women will challenge the views of the workshop leader early on, but then feel they are unable to be as dependent as they would like. Others will expose themselves too much early on and feel so vulnerable they are unable to continue. A lack of commitment from any group member who is repeatedly late or never puts up any of her own writing can eventually sabotage a group and a workshop leader may ask the group to address this early on.

Many women coming to a writing workshop worry that there will never be enough time to have their work read out and discussed. Others feel guilty when their work is discussed because they feel they are taking up too much of the group's time. Women often apologise for, or deride their work before it is read out and shared. The workshop leader ensures enough time for each woman's writing and helps members to present their work in a positive way.

Shared Workshop Leading

Two leaders can work well together by providing different ideas and responses to material. They can balance each other's strengths and weaknesses, offer support, and pick up on different aspects of the work which may have remained less developed with only one leader.

Sharing the running of a workshop can be difficult unless clear aims and objectives are established by discussing each stage of the workshop thoroughly beforehand and making a division of labour with some idea of the time allowed for each stage. Each leader will have a different pace and different interests. Being aware of these differences and any preoccupations or blind spots that you or your co–leader may have will enable a good working relationship to develop.

Working as a pair can also give leaders enough confidence to tackle subjects they might feel unhappy about handling alone. It can provide an opportunity to discuss what has occurred in a workshop with another professional, and to acknowledge feelings about workshop members which might otherwise remain unexpressed. The ability to maintain boundaries and yet be concerned and attentive to the stories women may tell in the workshop can often be strengthened by having another leader share some of the responsibility for acknowledging the amount of need that many women will bring to the workshop.

Glossary of Dramatic Techniques

1. Still Image/Tableau/Frozen Picture:

A group devises an image, represented by 'moulding' the bodies, gestures and facial expressions of members of the group to crystallise a moment, an idea or theme. An individual member who has a clear picture of the moment, 'sculpts' members into a tableau that is similar to a 'freeze–frame' on a video – the image is silent and unmoving. Picture–makers maintain their positions whilst the rest of the group look closely at, walk around and in between the picture, and give it a title, or make suggestions about its meaning.

Picture–makers allow observers to make their own interpretations until asked to reveal their starting–point. This technique requires reflection and analysis in selecting the image, and can represent complex issues in an accessible way. The whole group are free to interpret and to observe body language and power relationships. Contrasting images can also be used to represent hopes and fears about a situation, and contrasting titles can be given to emphasise the different ways an image can be read.

2. Mime:

Mime removes the pressure of dialogue and encourages exploration of body language and gesture. It can also emphasise the meanings of underlying actions, and can be useful for examining the subtext of a conversation/confrontation. Group members could mime a complex dialogue to understand the motivations behind it.

3. Taking on a role:

Taking on a role is not the same as acting a character. Women maintain their own voice and gestures, but alter their choice of tone and language as appropriate to the status, occupation, power relationships of the role they are playing. It is a demonstration of attitudes and behaviour rather than a performance.

4. Re–enactments:

An event that has actually happened is re–enacted in order to
a) reveal tensions and dynamics — group members may stop and discuss the action by using the command 'freeze'.
b) explore alternative endings — at the command 'freeze' group members may replace actors in the story to try out another way

of handling the situation, or may instruct actors on how to proceed. This process requires attention to detail, creative thinking and accuracy.

5. *Hotseating:*
A group member remains 'in role', preferably sitting in a specific chair, or hotseat, and the rest of the group asks questions of the character being role–played, in order to probe motivations further, build up a character's background situation/personal history. Best used as part of re–enactments, or role–playing a situation.

6. *Thought–tracking:*
A method of revealing characters' secret fears, hopes and desires that would not normally be revealed publicly. This can be used to deepen characterisation, and develop characters' "dream lives". Whilst a situation is being role–played, the leader can tap any character on the shoulder, the action freezes, and that character speaks her private thoughts and feelings. This is a counterpoint to what is publicly admitted and can be used to explore sub–text.

7. *Soundtracking:*
Soundtracking can be used in many ways and is best explained by examples:
a) Two groups prepare separate 'scenes'. The sound from one can then accompany the action from the other and vice versa. You can swap between the two scenes, like switching channels on television. Groups can prepare dialogue for a set piece of action.
b) Groups can invent sound collages to convey a mood or atmosphere e.g. each member of the group can come up with an individual sound to represent 'fear', which might be footsteps, breathing, the wind or animal cries. These are performed together to create a sound picture for the rest of the group.
Soundtracking brings another dimension to work on a particular theme or issue: sound can be particularly evocative. It can also be used to explore the distance between what is said, and what is shown.

8. *Drawing/visualising:*
Drawing can be used individually or collectively:
a) Individually:– each member of the group is asked to draw a picture for herself, e.g. of her first memory of a parent, or her idea of a monster or a heroine. If there is reluctance to share these personal images, then ask each woman to add three adjectives to her picture which she shares with the group as a starting–point for

25

discussion. Alternatively, stick the pictures on the wall and discuss them. Is the woman very large/small in relation to the monster/parent/sibling? Is she present or absent? Is she solid or sketchy?
b) Collectively: — the whole group draws a map/representation/collage, perhaps on a wallpaper roll spread out on the floor.

Drawing is particularly good for issues of self–image or self–representation. Pictures can summarise a whole range of feelings about an issue, conscious or unconscious and are a good way in to a personal theme, allowing a woman time and quiet to "access" a particular memory or feeling and a choice in whether she shares it or not.

9. Groupsize:

Varying the size of groups during a session, enables the leader to suit the group–size to the nature of the activity. For example, whole group discussion will usually be more general and objective, with the challenge of many different opinions, whilst pairwork will tend to be more intimate and allow discussion of a more personal nature. Whole group work will tend to be 'monitored' by the group leader, and can also be focussed by her, whilst pairwork will be determined by the two women concerned.

When planning a session, it is useful to begin and end in the whole group, to introduce and clarify themes, and to share problems and insights. Generally work intensifies the smaller the group and it is usual to go from large group introduction and 'warm–up' to small group or pairwork. This can be followed by reporting back and sharing insights, individual or paired writing tasks, ending with reading and discussing work in the whole group, to 'wind–down' as well as to get feedback.

Spending too long in any one size group can be counter– productive: women may be shy in a large group, but open up with one or two other women, whereas individual work can deepen the level of thought and commitment. On the other hand, personality clashes may occur, with one woman dominating the conversation, or being unable to respond supportively to a particular woman, or topic. In pair work there may always be one woman without a partner, who has to 'fit in' to another pair.

Whilst small groups allow discussion, and give more support to less confident women, allowing them to choose their level of contribution, members will also want to know what is going on in the rest of the group and will want to share and discuss ideas raised.

Workshop Exercises

Self-Assessment.

Aim: To identify skills, blocks and support systems.

Method:
1. Each member of the group should take four sheets of paper. Give each page one of the following titles: Skills, Problems, Support Systems, Ambitions.
2. Under each title, list your own
a) Skills — talents, qualities, what you're good at.
b) Problems — obstacles, difficulties, worries.
c) Support systems — things that keep you going, stimulants, good friends, family etc.
d) Ambitions — hopes and dreams.
3. Study your lists and write down three conclusions about whether you are managing to use your skills to achieve your ambitions. If you find it hard to identify skills this may suggest a lack of confidence.
If you find you have few support systems, you may be unwilling to seek help with problems.
If you have the same thing on two lists, e.g. a relationship may be supportive and problematic, or alcohol might be a support system and a problem, try and draw some conclusion about future plans.
4. Discussion of the group's feelings about this exercise.
Note: This exercise is designed to help writers identify those areas which may prevent them from using their talents to the full.
Lists should be made privately to enable total honesty.
Writers can then raise personal issues they wish to address and choose which issues they bring to the group for discussion afterwards.
This exercise can be combined with;

Becoming A Writer

Aim: To overcome internal fears and misgivings about being a writer.

Method:

1. Place three chairs facing each other in the centre of the room. One chair is for the "Novice Writer", the second is for the "Struggling Writer" and the third is for the "Famous Writer."

Notes on Roles: the Novice is in awe of the Famous Writer and idealistic about her future career. The Struggling Writer is experienced but is not successful enough to work full–time as a writer and is considering giving it up. The Famous Writer has been extremely successful, but has ceased to have anything new to say.

2. Three volunteers take on these roles. They improvise meeting at a conference where they discuss their writing with each other.

3. At any time the action can be stopped by the command "Freeze", and any other member of the group can swap into one of the roles and continue.

*Note:*This gives women the experience and status of being writers and the opportunity to air and discuss fears and anxieties which they may bring to the workshop. Problems like childcare, lack of confidence, money, education etc. can be shared as common difficulties and not as overwhelming obstacles to success.

Voice

Aim: To listen and tell stories and to explore the idea of a writer's "voice."

Method:

1. In pairs; A thinks of a recent story (from the news, real life or imaginary.)
2. A tells B her story. B listens and has to think of one word to describe how she feels, after hearing this story.
3. In the whole group, B reports back A's story and gives her "word". The leader may ask supplementary questions such as: What effect did the story have on the listener? Did the reporter improve on the story? What was best about the story? How would you describe the way A told the story? (The "voice".)
4. Discuss which stories were most effective. How much did the personality of the storyteller influence the listener? What made a story interesting? What made it boring?
5. Individually, choose one of the stories you have heard reported.
Imagine you have a story-teller with a unique way of relating the story — and think about what kind of language/dialect/colloquialisms/rhythm/imagery the story-teller might use.
6. Write the storytellers's version of the story.
7. Read and discuss.

Cliches, Lies and Exaggerations

Aim: To examine use and over-use of language. To facilitate writing dialogue.

Method:
1. Introduction and discussion of examples of "bad" dialogue. What is wrong? e.g. Over-explaining/too much information; use of dated or unintelligible slang; irrelevant chat; attempt at "poetic" language; obvious statements; lack of subtext; failure to demonstrate character attitude or emotion.
2. In small groups, devise a short scene from a soap opera, real or imaginary, to demonstrate the use of bad dialogue.
3. Share these with the whole group and discuss.
4. In the same groups try to rework the scenes into effective dialogue.
5. Share, or read aloud and discuss. What hooks did they use to engage interest? e.g. questions, strong reactions, interruptions, repetitions, force of persuasion. Was the dialogue in keeping with what we already know about the character's background and personality? Was it clichéd?
6. Discuss clichés and hackneyed language. Should we avoid them? How can we use them to effect?
7. In pairs, make lists of the clichéd dialogue associated with the following situations: Doctors and patients / teacher and pupils / lovers in love / rejected lovers. etc.
8. Read out the lists and then join with another pair and read out alternate lines from each list so that a new scene is created. How easy is it to swap cliches from one scene to another? Do they work better in a different context? Discuss.
9. Write on a slip of paper a line of dialogue which defines an attitude such as; "Never say die" or "Don't rock the boat."
10. Repeat with another slip of paper. Fold both slips and place them in a pile in the centre of the room.
11. Choose two different pieces of paper.
12. Two volunteers role-play a scene, which they devise by using one of the attitudes they have selected. Could we easily identify their character attitudes?
13. Write a short piece with two characters, using the two attitudes you have selected from the pile.
14. Share and discuss.

Room of One's Own

Aim: To look at the ways we use our space and to explore a writer's need for mental space.

Method:

1. Brainstorm the word "Space" for associations and write these on a large sheet in the centre of the room.

2. In pairs, describe your current room vividly — the colours, the smells, the sounds etc. Swap round.

3. Make a list of home improvements you'd like to make given an unlimited budget and share this list with your partner.

4. Think of a communal room in your present or past home and draw a picture from above of the way it is laid out.

5. Colour–code items and spaces in the room which are:

a) exclusively yours.

b) shared ownership.

c) never used by you.

6. Discuss how much of the room is yours? Which parts are shared? Which parts are essential to you? Which parts are the subject of conflict?

7. Imagine this conflict on a grander scale. Imagine a character who demands the right to a certain object or space. Write a story/poem/scene/monologue about this conflict.

8. Share and discuss. What space do you create for your writing?

9. Look back at the original associations for the word "Space". What other words might we add now?

NOTE: "...a woman must have money and a room of her own if she is to write fiction." Virginia Woolf *A Room of One's Own.* (Grafton Books)

Fear of Failure

Aim: To explore the fears we have about success and failure and to look at ways in which we sabotage ourselves and our work. To help build group cohesion.

Method: 1a) In pairs, A tells B a problem about work/writing. B demonstrates non–verbally through "Body Language" that she is not interested. Swap over.
b) Same pairs. This time, each partner expresses a great deal of concern and encouragement in acknowledging the other's problem.
2. Discuss these exercises and the ways in which people communicated their attitudes. What strategies were used to dismiss or encourage? How do we feel about positive/negative responses? Do we often receive a negative response which blocks us? Do we seek encouragement in the wrong places? How do we ensure we get the right response?
3. In groups of three, A and B hold an intimate conversation. Person C tries to interrupt, destroy, distract from the conversation A and B are having. When C has succeeded in steering the conversation in her own direction, stop and swap round.
4. Discuss the strategies that were used to sabotage the interaction between A and B. How did it feel being excluded? How easy was it to sabotage A and B?
5. In a circle, the whole group does a round of:
a) I could sabotage this group by....
b) I could help this group by....
c) I sabotage my work by...
d) I could help my work by...
6. A volunteer is asked to "mould" or "sculpt" a frozen picture/tableau of a memory they have of an incident involving sabotage or self-sabotage. They use the other members of the group to create their picture.
7. The rest of the group walk round the picture and comment on what they see, offering titles for it. Members can swap in and out of the picture so that everyone can see it.
8. Discuss what thoughts and feelings were evoked. How much do we sabotage ourselves in our daily lives?

Self-Censorship

Aim: to identify and overcome a writer's personal blocks with/without a specific piece of work.

Method:
1. A volunteer takes a chair in the centre of the circle. The leader asks her to choose members of the group to 'act out' her blocks.
i.e. if the woman in the hotseat feels that a particular teacher at school, or a parent, sibling, favourite writer is getting in the way of her writing, she chooses another member of the group to represent each person she has mentioned (CENSORS).
2. Women playing the censors then stand around her and place their hands lightly on her shoulders, and the volunteer explains to them the inhibiting attitudes of the people they represent.
3. The volunteer then begins to talk about her current project, or her writing in general, or her feelings about being a writer. Each time she says anything that might offend/alienate/upset one of the censors, they press on her shoulder and she must ask them what she has said to offend them, and then argue against their censorship, convincing them to remove their hand and sit down.
4. The process continues until each censor has been confronted and has removed their pressure.
5. Discuss.
NOTE: A volunteer may choose censors for a variety of reasons: either, a friend/relative/colleague who specifically disparages her writing, or :
— a favourite writer who is so good the volunteer feels that there is no point in competing (this is also a good exercise for establishing a personal voice).
— a family member whose attitudes are important to the woman, and who is discouraging, or who specifically/implicitly censors a certain subject area e.g. a parent may not like their daughter writing about her sexual experiences.
This exercise is adapted from a workshop given originally by Jules Wright. (The Women's Playhouse Trust).

Violence

Aim: To explore a theme using drama techniques.

Method:
1. Draw a picture of an act of violence.
2. Describe it with three adjectives.
3. Take on the adjectives yourself in a round e.g. "I am violent", "I am arbitrary", "I am political". etc. Go round the group three times and hear all the adjectives.
4. In pairs, A takes on the role of aggressor, B the role of counsellor. A speaks about the act of violence she has committed against another, as if for the first time (in role), while B listens.
5. B reports back what she has been told, to the group. How difficult was it to take on the role of aggressor? Did you modify your original act of violence when asked to do this? Is violence a taboo for women? Where do women direct their anger? Discuss.
6. In the same pairs A and B reverse roles. This time, recalling the original adjectives, B has been violent, but she is 'the victim' herself — not an outsider, and the act is more one of self-destruction. A takes on the role of counsellor hearing the story for the first time.
7. A reports back to the whole group. How were these stories different? Was it easier to identify with the violence? What was the attitude of the woman to her violence? How did this compare with the attitudes of the aggressors in the preceding exercise? Discuss.
8. Choose to be either the aggressor or the victim. Write a piece about violence.
9. Share these and discuss.

The Personal and the Political

Aim: To discover ways of transforming personal experience into political experience.

Method:

1. Discussion about where the personal and the political overlap e.g. 'a woman's right to choose/abortion'.

2. Which writers are successful at blending or juxtaposing the personal and the political? e.g. Alice Walker, Caryl Churchill, Sarah Daniels. Discuss passages/instances.

3. Think about the power structure within your own family. Imagine it to be the power structure of a State. Leader may need to discuss these ideas further and give examples.

4. Volunteers each present a tableau, using members of the group to represent the power structure/hierarchy of the imaginary State. Members will present slightly different tableaux e.g. a colony, a matriarchy, a dictatorship, a country in the grip of civil war. Discuss each tableau and find a word to describe the kind of State depicted, and define the ways in which power is distributed within it.

5. Look at Churchill's *Cloud Nine* or Pinter's *Mountain Language*. Read and discuss a part of one of these plays. What kind of power structure does the play suggest in terms of:
a) the State? (b) the Family?

6. Write your own piece, where the personal and the political are intertwined.

7. Share and discuss.

Fathers

Aim: To explore feelings and ideas about: fatherhood/authority/success/social identity.

Method:
1. Draw a picture of an early memory of your father/grandfather/a father figure.
2. Think of three adjectives to describe this person and write them below the picture.
3. Share some of the adjectives with the group.
4. Divide into small groups to discuss and share memories. Some women may not feel able to do this unless they work in a pair with a trusted partner.
5. Each group chooses one woman's memory to sculpt in the form of a frozen picture.
6. Come together, and then groups choose one by one to share the frozen picture.
7. Each picture is given a title by the group.
8. Ask for one group to update their picture. Beginning with the first frozen picture positioning, the picture-maker moves and changes the elements to represent a more recent memory.
9. Discuss what changed, e.g. power relationships, relative size, body language, distance, attitudes etc. What did the pictures evoke for the audience and the participants?
10. Write a story/scene/poem/monologue about a father.
11. Share and discuss.
12. Looking back at the pictures and adjectives, discuss how our relationships with fathers may affect our feelings toward male authority, our attitudes to our careers, and our sense of self.
NOTE: This session can be adapted to explore relationships with mothers, sisters etc.

Subverting Fairytales

Aim: To find alternate endings for age-old stories. To look at the way feminism has changed our perceptions.

Method:
1. Read the traditional story *The Little Mermaid.*
2. Read *The Pangs of Love* by Jane Gardam*.
3. Divide into two groups. Group A prepares an improvised scene from *The Little Mermaid.* Group B prepares an improvised scene from the *The Pangs of Love.*
4. Group A presents their scene once and Group B watch it with a view to adding a new soundtrack to it in line with their author's view of the world.
5. Group B discuss the new soundtrack and then ask Group A to re-run the scene silently. Group B provide the sound effects, dialogue, music, narration etc.
6. Repeat with the scene Group B have prepared. This time Group A devise a new soundtrack from the perspective of the Hans Andersen original. Group B re-run the scene with the new soundtrack.
7. Discuss the effect of this counterpointing. Discuss how Jane Gardam changed the original. What kind of language/style/characterisation did she employ? Make a list of techniques that were used by the groups and the writer to subvert the original story, e.g. parody, bathos, exaggeration, repetition etc.
8. Choose a fairytale you know well.
9. Write a new version of it from a different perspective. Try using some of the techniques you have listed, try updating it or changing the setting. What kind of ending do you want for your story?
10. Share these and discuss.
NOTE: For further reading about fairy tales see:
   The Pangs of Love and other stories by Jane Gardam.
(Also included in *Close Company* collection [Virago]).
The Uses of Enchantment by Bruno Bettelheim.
The Bloody Chamber by Angela Carter.

Developing Complex Characters

Aim: To deepen character.

Method:
1. Discuss opposition and conflict in stories, in soaps, in recent plays.
2. Invent a character with an aim or mission in life.
3. Invent obstacles to this character's success on three levels:
i) Conflict with self
ii) Conflict with family and friends
iii) Conflict with society/authority/environment.
4. Invent situations in which the character will come into conflicts on each of these three levels. The choices the character makes in these situations are often known as 'turning-points.'
5. What is the outcome of these choices? Do they lead to further complications and difficulties for the character to resolve before they can achieve their aim? Do they succeed too easily?
6. Make up a chart of the character's journey along the lines of a board game (Snakes and Ladders/Monopoly). Draw in alternate choices for your character at each stage — the moves s/he doesn't make in your story, but could have made.
7. Choose one moment from your chart and hot-seat a member of the group who role-plays their character at that moment of the story.
8. Discuss this moment and what we learn about the character from it. Look at the character's chart. Does it bear out what we expect of her/him?
9. Repeat with other members of the group.
10. Write this scene, portraying the moment of choice for the character.
11. Share and discuss.

Resolutions

Aim: To examine how an ending fulfils emotional needs in an audience and resolves the major conflicts of the story.

Method:
1. Think of a good and a bad ending to a play or film.
Plays with different kinds of endings such as *Saved*, *Hedda Gabler*, *Waiting for Godot*, *Top Girls* might be discussed.
2. Compile a list of criteria for good endings.
Did the ending demonstrate the central idea of the play/film? Was it ambiguous or ironic perhaps?
3. In pairs, choose a central idea for a play/film by remembering a time when your ideas or attitudes about a person or an issue suddenly changed. Tell your partner what event made you change your mind in this way. Swap.
4. Write an account of your partner's story.
5. Take turns reading this back to your partner.
6. Write a piece from an opposite perspective to the one you now hold, that will argue with the account that your partner has drawn.
7. Share this counter-view with your partner, in turn.
8. Using the two different accounts and opposing views that you and your partner have created, write the scene in which these two opponents confront each other and fight it out to the finish. You have written the final scene of a play.
9. Share and discuss these in the whole group.Can we guess what the central idea is and what the counter idea is? Is the scene successful in resolving the conflict? Does it leave us feeling we want to know more?
10. In *Top Girls* the final scene demonstrates the central idea that 'women's success is built on the backs of other women and often at the expense of having chidren.' Is the conflict resolved? Is there a winner and a loser? Discuss.

COLLABORATION

Vinegar Tom
by Caryl Churchill

Early in 1976 I met some of the Monstrous Regiment, who were thinking they would like to do a play about witches; so was I, though it's hard now to remember what ideas I was starting from. I think I had already read *Witches, Midwives and Nurses* by Barbara Ehrenreich and Deirdre English. Certainly it had a strong influence on the play I finally wrote.

Soon I met the whole company to talk about working with them. They gave me a list of books they had read and invited me to a rehearsal of *Scum*. I left the meeting exhilarated. My previous work had been completely solitary — I never discussed my ideas while I was writing or showed anyone anything earlier than a final polished draft. So this was a new way of working, which was one of its attractions. Also a touring company, with a wider audience; also a feminist company — I felt briefly shy and daunted, wondering if I would be acceptable, then happy and stimulated by the discovery of shared ideas and the enormous energy and feeling of possibilities in the still new company.

I was about to do a play for Joint Stock, who excited me for some of the same reasons, some different. There wasn't a lot of time, and the two plays, *Vinegar Tom* and *Light Shining in Buckinghamshire,* overlapped both in time and ideas. All I knew at this point about the Joint Stock project was that it was going to be about the English Revolution in the 1640's, what people had wanted from it, and particularly the millenial expectations of the Ranters. A lot of what I was learning about the period, religion, class, the position of women, was relevant to both plays.

I rapidly left aside the interesting theory that witchcraft had existed as a survival of supressed pre–Christian religions and went instead for the theory that witchcraft existed in the minds of its persecutors, that 'witches' were a scapegoat in times of stress like Jews and blacks. I discovered for the first time the extent of Christian teaching against women and saw the connections between medieval attitudes to witches and continuing attitudes to women in general. The women accused of witchcraft were often those on the edge of society, old, poor, single, sexually unconventional; the old herbal medical tradition of the cunning woman was suppressed by the rising professionalism of the male doctor. I didn't base the play on any precise historical events, but set it rather loosely in the seventeenth century, partly because it was the time of the last major English witchhunts, and partly because the social upheavals, class changes, rising professionalism and great hardship among the poor were the context of the kind of witchhunt I wanted to write about; partly of course because it was the period I was already reading about for Joint Stock. One of the things that struck me reading the detailed accounts of witch trials in Essex (*Witchcraft in Tudor and Stuart England, Macfarlane*) was how petty and everyday the witches' offences were, and how different the atmosphere of actual English witchhunts seemed to be from my received idea, based on slight knowledge of the European witchhunts and films and fiction, of burnings, hysteria and sexual orgies. I wanted to write a play about witches with no witches in it; a play not about evil, hysteria and possession by the devil but about poverty, humiliation and prejudice, and how the women accused of witchcraft saw themselves.

I met Monstrous Regiment again, talked over the ideas I had so far, and found the same aspects of witchcraft appealed to them too. Then I went off and wrote a first draft of the play, very quickly, in about three days. I may have written one or two songs at this stage but not all of them. The company were happy to accept this first draft and leave rewriting till after my work with Joint Stock, which was lucky as in May I started the Joint Stock workshop. In the autumn I met Monstrous Regiment again. Helen Glavin had been working on the music for the songs during the summer. I worked on the text again, expanding it slightly. It was only at this stage that Josefina Cupido joined the company and I wrote in the character of Betty, who didn't exist before and who filled a need that had come up in discussion for a character under pressure to make a conventional marriage. It was a very enjoyable co–operation with the company. My habit of solitary working and shyness at showing what I wrote at an early stage had been wiped out by the even greater self–exposure in Joint Stock's method of work.

And our shared view of what the play was about and our commitment to it made rewriting precise and easy. By the time *Traps* was done in January 1977 it seemed more than a year since I had written it. Though I still wanted to write alone sometimes, my attitude to myself, my work and others had been basically and permamently changed.

Caryl Churchill. 1982

Originally printed as an introduction to *Vinegar Tom* in Caryl Churchill's *Plays: One*. Reprinted by permission of Methuen Drama.

Television: Writing by Committee
by Jill Hyem

One of the dictionary definitions of the word collaborate is "to work with the enemy." Sometimes the collaboration process in television feels exactly like that to the writer.

Collaboration with other writers or members of a production team can be at best a deeply rewarding and stimulating process, at worst a nightmare of conflicting egos. I have experienced both and many shades between. I suppose, did I not enjoy to some extent the give and take of collaborative work, I would have long since crawled away from the field of television and tried my hand at writing novels.

I started writing in radio, where my happiest collaborations, both with writers and producers, took place. As co–creator (with Alan Downer) of *Waggoners Walk* (the daily serial which ran during the 70's) I worked for most of its duration with a team of four writers — two women, two men. There were no script editors as there are of necessity in television soaps. The four writers, together with the producer and appropriate story advisors, met regularly to plan storylines. We would discuss character and story continuity on the phone and at "handover meetings", but we were given as much creative freedom as was possible within the restrictions of the genre. The team of writers complimented each other. They were generous and supportive. The atmosphere was non–competitive. This is not to say we did not argue frequently and heatedly during meetings, but we let our conflicting views become the conflicts of the characters rather than a destructive force within the group. It was a happy and productive team. When the programme was axed without warning in the 1979 cutbacks we all suffered severe withdrawal symptoms.

Side by side with my series work I had been writing single plays in radio, anxious as I was to preserve an individual voice. This is one of the dangers of team–writing for series where an overall style has to be maintained. I was very fortunate to work closely with two women producers during this time. (Jane Morgan and Kay Patrick who still directs my radio plays.) They both involved themselves with the script from conception to completion and both involved me in all the production processes. I was always consulted

44

about casting, always made welcome in the studio where my comments were sought and valued. I was acknowledged as the prime creator.

I know now that I was living in Cloud Cuckoo Land...

Television — particularly in the field of Series and Serials means working by committee and the writer can only too easily become an absentee member of that committee once the script is delivered. A sympathetic script–editor can make sure that the writer is considered and involved at all stages, but only too often script–editors are just another link in the destructive Whispering Game which distances a writer from his/her work. The director is invariably brought in after the script has been completed and has possibly been through several drafts. He or she (usually a he) seldom cares about the writer's intent (if indeed he knows what it is) and the producer rarely does anything to ease this potentially stressful situation.

On the second series of *Wish Me Luck* I was not even invited to meet the director, let alone to discuss with him the two opening episodes which I had written and which introduced the new characters. This, in spite of the fact that I had co– created the series (with Lavinia Warner) and written most of the first series. It is not entirely surprising that a series which set out to explore the role of women agents and the effects of espionage work on their lives soon became a traditional resistance adventure series with an all–male production team and mostly male writers. The ratings were no higher for this change of gear and the audience appreciation figures lower than on the original series.

I had a similar experience on *Howard's Way* for which I was the original writer. (I wrote five of the first seven episodes.) A cynical male production team — more concerned with cash and catamarans than characters — soon caused me to seek fresh waters. It is interesting to note that although other women writers were commissioned to write episodes over the subsequent series none of their scripts were used. Jan Harvey, the leading actress, has publically bemoaned the fact that there had not been any women writers since the original series. She felt her part had suffered from the fact.

Tenko, which I co–wrote with Anne Valery, was a very different experience. The story was about a group of women internees in a Japanese POW Camp. It ran for three series and was followed by

45

a two–hour Christmas special. The two producers and five directors were all men, but with a female creator and prison camp advisor, two determined women writers and a wonderful cast of actresses whose intentions were the same as ours, the series stayed mainly on course.

There is, it often appears, a conspiracy in television to keep writers and actors (and indeed writers and directors) away from each other. We are told we must be "protected from them." It is true that some actors are incapable of objectivity or of seeing characters or stories other than in terms of the length of their own scenes. But this has seldom been the case in my experience. One of my first experiences of working with a "star" was with Wendy Craig on *Nanny*. No–one could have been more eager to discuss the character or more encouraging while I was writing. I had a similar experience more recently with Victoria Tennant who starred in my dramatisation of Barbara Taylor Bradford's *Act of Will*.

Tenko's popularity was largely because of the audience's identification with the characters. Anne Valery and I collaborated closely throughout. We would spend days together discussing character development. We also discussed their characters with the main actresses, though this was not encouraged by the producer! I remember meeting Stephanie Beecham in secret to discuss the manner of her screen death. I wanted it to be a play about euthanasia and I wanted Stephanie to be involved in the evolution of the story since the character of Rose was hers as much as mine.

I know the *Tenko* actresses found working together a unique collaborative experience which forged deep friendships. They spoke on many occasions of the relief of not having to worry about their looks, of being able to concentrate on the real priorities as a team. No–one was given billing throughout the series. It was the decision of the producer (Ken Riddington) that it should be a joint venture. And such it was.

A collaboration of any kind involves a degree of compromise. This has to be accepted, but it need not lead to the "take–the–money–and–run" attitude of compliance of some television writers. I always know my sticking–points and when the compromising has to stop. For this I am said by some people to be "difficult" and by others to have "integrity."

I have to say that on the whole I have found women directors and producers easier to collaborate with than their male counterparts. (Although there are notable exceptions.) They seem more honest, more open to ideas, less likely to indulge in the power games that are a feature of television.

One of the happiest productions I worked on was a Miss Marple dramatisation (*At Bertram's Hotel*) directed by Mary McMurray who has an extraordinary gift for being able to create a "company" feel such as one experiences sometimes in the theatre. She made a point of bringing everyone together some while before rehearsals started, so that one had the rare luxury of discussing the project with the designers, wardrobe and make–up artists, sound and camera people as well as the actors. Far from losing control (the fear of so many directors) it gained her the respect and trust of all concerned.

I think it is significant that one of the most highly praised and distinguished pieces of television drama in recent times — *Oranges are not the Only Fruit* — was written, produced and directed by three young women. (Jeanette Winterson, Phillipa Giles and Beeban Kidron.) A very rich collaboration.

Equal Terms by Jill Hyem (Samuel French.)
Remember Me by Jill Hyem in *Giles Cooper Awards: Best Radio Plays of 1979.* (B.B.C. Publications.)

Writing with Actors...
or....The Playwright gets out of her Garret
by Bryony Lavery

There is an illusion that writers are solitary souls... never happier than when they are sitting hunched over typewriters in their lofty garrets high above the hurly–burly of the common throng. While this may be true of some poets and novelists.... this is not the case with the playwright.

She chooses a form of expression which is not complete until it has been passed carefully through the minds and bodies of a director, actors, designer, musical director, stage managers, lighting designer, administrators, publicists, audience and finally, oh bitter pill, critics. Each cook adds another ingredient to this peculiar piece of cooking called a play. And while it is true that the first ingredient is often the text... this is by no means necessarily the most enjoyable method of playwriting.

Actors are one of the most miserably under–used resources in British Theatre today. Nine times out of ten they are the last people to be employed when a play is being put on. They are then chosen because of their apparent ability to portray one character. One time out of ten they are allowed in at an earlier stage of the process...and then...let Joy Be Unconfined! Their ability to play ...to take what is in the mind and translate it into action, pictures and plot...to turn the ordinary into the extraordinary, passivity into activity, the unsayable into the do–able...is such a splendid gift to a writer of plays that one would be a BIG NIT not to take full advantage of it. During my time as a playwright I have had whole armfuls of gifts from the actors of Monstrous Regiment, The National Theatre of Brent, Female Trouble, Theatre Centre, The Wandsworth Warmers, Clean Break and many, many others but I only have four pages here and space is small. They have provided everything from the entire plot of a play, to characters I would never have dreamed up in a million years to the most exquisite detail of dialogue and behaviour.

Here is my blueprint for starting a play with actors: Choose an ENORMOUS country of experience. Think Big. Travel in the mind is cheapest, but it's up to you. With Monstrous Regiment we once chose the entire study of Evolution, another time the Wild

West. With Clean Break, we started with The Prison System. With The National Theatre of Brent we went from The Zulu Wars through India to The Wagnerian Ring Cycle. (We once rejected Wuthering Heights as "too small"). Find somewhere in your head you've never been to, know a little about, and wouldn't mind a fact–finding mission to, and go. You will be carrying your own baggage of experience and emotion with you, so don't worry about NOT WRITING OUTSIDE YOUR OWN EXPERIENCE (Classic Dumb Advice From Mean–Spirited Kitchen–Sink Minds.)

Talk your Actors into going with you. This will not be hard as most actors worth their salt do not want to play themselves, more or less, sitting on chairs at tables in rooms rather like their own. They like to wear Givenchy dresses, tattered rags, cowgirl outfits, wigs, baggy trousers, red noses and wings. (Don't you?) They want to fall madly in love, kill someone, feed a baby, work on the railroad, discover a cure for cancer and fly by their own device. (Don't you?) They want to be Gods, Devils, Lovers, Murderers, Plotters, Thieves, Children and Aged Crones. (Don't you?)

As a Woman Playwight you have a duty to create plays which a) Tell exciting stories about women, b) provide exciting parts for the thousands of brilliant and under–employed women actors in this country and c) do shows which we miserably–under–catered –for 52 per cent of the population scour The Entertainments Guide weekly for!

Gather Good Actors about you. There are many of these. Go scouting for them. Ask them. They can only say No. Say "We are going to explore Death, The International Monetary System, Betrayal, The Circus, Astronomy, The Private Life of the Crab Louse, The Sea, Queens, Copulation, Australia"....whatever you have decided.

Don't talk too much. Do.

Set up scenarios, games, rules....bits of play that might alter your perception, create a different reality, hurl you into a different century, transport you onto another planet. Get every–one to come in as the character they have always wanted to play .....but no–one has yet written the play with her or him in it. You might find a Chinese female pirate, half a pantomime horse, Boadicea, Emily Dickinson and a Rottweiler turning up. Put them in scenes. Make them play games. See what they do. Why not? There are plays in which Royal Princes talk to Gravediggers, Kings go mad with Fools, Women from different centuries sit down for supper together.

Give them a story you like. Get them to do it in different styles...Playschool, Grand Opera, Greek Tragedy, Western, Hollywood Musical, the style you perceive as yours, Shakespearian, any novel...each playing will reveal more...the story grows and changes...

Scour books by Keith Johnstone, Viola Spolin, Stanislavski, Micheal Chekov...any books about Theatre Games and devising processes and ways in which actors work and adapt and use the ones which appeal to you to open up another can of worms.

Make up your own methods of turning what's in the mind into how bodies behave.

Excite and interest yourself and it will excite and interest others.

All the books you have read, the things you have seen, done, felt, all the things you have thought will be added to by the particular make–up of an actor's brain. Alfred Hitchcock said that Actors were cattle. Wrong, Alfred. They are people who have read a lot, done a lot, been through a lot. They don't just roam about and moo.

So you will be given idea after idea, character upon character, story upon story, voice upon voice. Then you can climb up to your lofty garret...you walk about among your rich collection of actors' gifts...and you find the structure which will show them off to full advantage. And you write them a CRACKING GOOD PLAY.

Happy Writing!

Origin of the Species by Bryony Lavery in *Plays by Women* Vol. 6 ed. by Micheline Wandor (Methuen Drama.)

Masks and Faces ed. by Bryony Lavery (Macmillan)

Caving In
by Ayshe Raif

I can quite honestly say that, were it not for the encouragement and collaborative efforts of the people I'm about to mention, my play *Caving In* (produced in May 1989) would never have been completed.

By mid 1988 my confidence was at its lowest ebb and I felt I'd lost my ability to write. I had a meeting with Tony Craze, himself a writer and the Artistic Director of the Soho Poly Theatre, where I'd had plays previously produced. He offered me a commission and said I was to write whatever I wanted. I was immensely grateful, but it wasn't long after this meeting that I rang him to say I was going to return the commissioning fee and that, really, I couldn't write anymore. He was wonderful. He encouraged me not to give up and suggested I attend some workshops at the theatre. Four writers, a number of actors and a director would meet on alternating Sundays for four all–day sessions for the benefit of the writers involved. Each writer would have two separate half–day sessions.

Claire Grove was the director running the sessions and we'd met before, so that was good. I managed to produce a very rough draft which I forwarded to Claire and on the 5th November 1988 I attended the first session with some trepidation.

The actors were Jacquetta May, Peter Shorey, Lynne Verall and Simon Wright. The first thing they did was to read the play to us and then we discussed it at some length. Just having a group of people focussed on the play and the characters was almost stimulus enough, but then they improvised and opened it out for me. And of course the things that didn't work were soon obvious. It was a great day and I went home and got down to work, no longer spending time wondering if I could write or not. People had given a lot of input and rekindled that excitement I used to feel when working on a play. Not only had their criticism been constructive, but they also gave generously of that precious necessity — praise.

By the second session on the 10th December, I'd produced another draft. This session again began with a reading, followed by a more subtle dissection of the play and it's faults. Many questions were raised that hadn't been addressed in the script, but

51

again there was praise enough to encourage me to continue. Shortly after that session I submitted an official first draft to Tony and in due course we had a meeting.

I remember it as a relaxed conversation, but when I look back at the notes I'd made immmediately afterwards, I realise how Tony's gentle questions and comments were actually frank and incisive and a tremendous amount of help to me at the time. I realised I had a big gaping hole in the play, which I'd padded out with fun but rather irrelevant fantasy sequences. Without them I didn't have a lot left. So I took them out and got down to my research. It wasn't long before I hit on a new element which fixed the focus of the play squarely on the main character and things began to come together, but there still was a long way to go. An almost complete re–write for a start, which is where Claire Grove re–entered the picture.

I'd enjoyed working with Claire and asked for her to be the eventual director and Tony had agreed. It was to be a while before her contract materialised but even so I plagued her mercilessly with phone calls and whimpers for praise and encouragement, which she duly gave. She was constantly supportive and still is. Claire is an excellent director with a no–nonsense approach to her work which I appreciate and admire. We had many meetings and discussions and eventually the second draft was completed in April 1989. The work didn't stop there either. I was present for about two–thirds of the rehearsal period (with actors Diane Bull, Phillip Joseph, Simon Wright and Mona Bruce) where a lot of cutting and re–writing was done. The cutting process actually carried on till Press Night, but I think we were all happy with the final results and the notices were excellent.

Now, I'm not saying that anyone wrote the play for me, or that it didn't take a tremendous amount of work on my part, but I doubt that I'd have found my way to that final stage without the generous input and support of the people around me, not least Claire Grove who made me feel that she never for a moment doubted my ability.

I feel tremedously honoured for the treatment I received. Unfortunately it's becoming increasingly rare for writers to be coaxed, cajoled and encouraged to produce their best work. Shortage of money and commercialism have made the theatre into much more of a business than an art world. If you don't have the goods, there's a dozen people behind you who do, is the prevalant attitude.

But is it true? How often do people bemoan the lack of good new plays? Writers aren't salesmen with boxes of pristine samples under their arms. Our post production scripts often bear little resemblance to our first submitted drafts and in this way all produced plays are a collaborative effort. And the play only comes fully to life with the collaborative response of an audience.

All writers need stimulus and support. I was lucky enough to have workshops, actors, a good director and a sympathetic person to commission me. It should be the norm, but it's an almost unique luxury these days.

If you ever get that sort of opportunity, you should grab it with both hands — and fast!

Caving In by Ayshe Raif was first produced at the Soho Poly Theatre, London, in May 1989. It was subsequently adapted for the BBC Radio Four's Monday Night Theatre and broadcast on March 12th 1990. Both productions were directed by Claire Grove. *Caving In* will be published by Methuen in Autumn 1990.

Dramaturgy
by Cheryl Robson

In Britain, there have been few attempts to make use of the Dramaturge in the same way as she/he is employed in Europe. A strategy group was set up by Tony Craze at the Soho Poly Theatre to try and get support for a programme of regional dramaturges, who would be responsible for new writing initiatives within their areas.

People seemed to be confused by the term "dramaturge" and often asked what does a Dramaturge do? How is it different from the job of a Literary Manager?

I had the chance to talk to Jorg Mihan, a Dramaturge from the Berliner Ensemble and asked him to outline the background and nature of his job.

He told me that a theatre building in West Germany often houses theatre, ballet and orchestral companies. Each of these companies employs two or three dramaturges who work with directors on different projects. The Berliner Ensemble employs four dramaturges and tours its productions to around fifty venues. There are 3/4 productions a year.

He believes the job of a dramaturge is:

1. To discuss the play with the director and the writer and to act as the director's artistic/literary/scientific assistant at rehearsals.
2. To act as an advisor/critic at all stages of production.
3. To collaborate with the director on decisions affecting the preparation, conception, design etc. of the production.
4. To act as a link between the playwright and the theatre.
5. To follow a script through from receipt to production.
6. To be responsible for all publicity/publications in connection with the production.
7. To write programme notes and educational material relating to the production.
8. To give introductions to the audience and to arrange student discussions afterwards.
9. To read and evaluate scripts. (Only 5/10 scripts arrive each month).

What kind of person is employed as a Dramaturge?

A person with a background in Theatre Science or Theatre History, often a recent graduate from university.

What Jorg Mihan told me was surprising. He was not involved in running writers' workshops or making contacts with new writers outside of the theatre. New writers were mostly introduced to the Berliner Ensemble via publishers. There were few writers' workshops in Berlin and the only course he knew of, concerned with the training of theatre writers, was a course at the Herder Institute.

This contrasts enormously with the work of dramaturges in this country. North West Playwrights' Workshops, an independent project set up and run by playwrights from the Theatre Writers' Union has been using dramaturges in the process of workshopping scripts and developing them for a series of rehearsed readings before a public audience. They describe the role of the dramaturge in this way:

> The dramaturge's main function is to be the writer's friend. For many writers, the Workshops will be their first experience of working with a professional company; others may be new to theatre. Even more experienced writers will be anxious: Will the actors like the script? Will the director want to do it in a public performance? The role of the dramaturge is to minimise this anxiety by working with the writer on the script before the workshops begin, discussing with the writer and director what the writer wants out of the process and by protecting the writer in rehearsals. The dramaturge should let the writer know from the start that good plays are generally re-written.

What kind of person does the job?

An experienced writer.

The idea of an experienced writer as dramaturge was also taken up by South–West Arts who employed John Downie as a regional dramaturge. His contact was not with one theatre, but with many theatres throughout the region and the possibility of satisfying the needs of so many different artistic directors must have made the job enormously difficult.

Recently, we saw some of the work which he developed with writers in Bristol, performed at the Riverside Studios in London as part of the Bristol Express' *The Play's the Thing* series. Entitled *Living in Interesting Times* the six short pieces selected from over twice that number, demonstrated a diversity of style and subject matter, both funny and moving.

This showcasing of the work occurred only because of the involvement of Bristol Express' Artistic Director, Andy Jordan in the Bristol workshops and his belief in the value of these short pieces. Bristol Express Theatre Company is a company committed to new writing which has presented over forty plays in *The Play's The Thing* since 1986. Over one third of these have been produced professionally, seven by the company with plans to produce a further four.

Bristol Express does not employ writers to act as dramaturges, although there is the option for involvement in rehearsals on the part of the Literary Manager. But a Literary Manager's job differs distinctly from the work of a dramaturge. In detailing some of the work I've undertaken as the Literary Manager for the company since October 1988, I hope to give some insight into the nature of the job of Literary Manager.

My first task was to try and locate the many scripts submitted to the company over the years and to institute an effective system of reading and evaluating these scripts and returning those which were considered unsuitable for the company. Tracking down the many different script–readers was sometimes a problem. Reasons for not reading/returning a script were often imaginative: "I've had my briefcase stolen" or "I've been in America/on tour/ill for six months."

Following detailed discussions about shortlisted scripts, which several members of the company had read, the programme for the fourth *The Play's the Thing* was agreed and the series was presented from January to March 1989 at the Lyric Theatre in Hammersmith. Three very good plays by women made it a strong programme.

The poet Carol Rumens' first play *But Svoboda's a Russian Word,* had been developed by Bristol Express' workshopping process before being given a staged reading. We were hoping to do her next play too, but her work was seen and snapped up by Pascal Theatre Company who produced *Nearly Siberia* a few months later in both Newcastle and at the Soho Poly Theatre in London.

Sarah Aicher's playreading of *Heaven* went ahead, despite the tragic death of the writer and her boyfriend, the actor Matthew Paul Freeman on the PanAm flight that became known as the Lockerbie disaster. There was a heavy atmosphere as we filed into

56

the theatre that day along with Sarah's family and friends to see and hear this vivid first play about the plight of London's dispossessed.

Claire Booker's *The Devil and Stepashka,* an adaptation of a Tolstoy short story, became the surprise hit of the season. It was taken up by another company and went on to successful productions on the Edinburgh Fringe and at Hampstead's New End Theatre.

The current *The Play's the Thing* festival is unfolding new and varied plays as I write this piece. Among the offerings this year is Jean Binnie's play *Boudicca's Victory* which was adapted from a radio play and received an exciting workshop production, directed by Richard Osborne. This is an epic play about war in Ancient Britain which deserves a full production, but with a cast of around twenty it may have difficulty finding a producer to take it on. Without financial backing, there is little more the company can do for the writer, despite a strong belief in the value of the play as theatre. Without realistic funding, New Writing Festivals are in danger of becoming a self–serving process that is a substitute for professional production.

The North West Playwrights' Workshops have been successful in setting up schemes so that the writers who have contributed to their Playreading Festivals can go on to work professionally in the theatre. They have encouraged the theatres in the northwest to produce new plays and take on the plays which have been given workshopped productions. They have also joined with theatres and funding bodies to plan new writing initiatives in the region including four new residencies for playwrights in Greater Manchester Theatres and four new commissions to writers whose plays have previously been workshopped. Most of this has been achieved by playwrights coming together and working voluntarily on the project, and after several years of organising and fundraising, they have finally received the resources to pay a Project Co–ordinator.

Why did the playwrights in this region feel the need to do something for new writing? Surely, the theatres employed Literary Managers, reading and responding to new scripts? The truth is that Literary Managers in Britain are often required to adminstrate a company's script–reading system and only rarely are they involved in running workshops for new writers or for more established writers the theatre has commissioned in the past. They are often involved in communicating with literary agents, commissioning writers and maintaining contacts with those writers through various redraftings of scripts prior to production. Once the play has been produced, there is little follow–up unless a new commission is in the offing. This helps to increase the isolation of writers who often feel unconnected to theatres, even when those theatres have benefited from their work.

Literary Managers also lack the status and power of their European counterparts when it comes to being involved in artistic decisions about the production. They are often bogged down in getting the hundreds of scripts read which have been submitted to the company. If they find scripts which they believe are important and interesting they can do no more than try and persuade their Artistic Director to take up the script. The tastes and values of the Artistic Director usually dictate the company's producing and commissioning policies.

In the majority of cases, men are employed as Artistic Directors (See: The Women's Playhouse Trust's report *What Share of the Cake?*) by companies increasingly pressurised by a lack of finance to come up with a safe and commercially rewarding programme of work. In some theatres, decisions about scripts are taken, not only by Artistic Directors, Associate Directors and Literary Managers, but also by Marketing and Financial Controllers.

The chances for new writing and women's writing become slender in this kind of financial atmosphere where theatres fall back on revivals and the classics and cut themselves off from the creative roots of their own communities.

The regional dramaturge scheme is a way round this. If new writing initiatives are given sufficient resources by the regional arts associations, to enable playwrights to present work in the form of readings, and workshop productions, with a commitment to develop scripts for full production, then new writers can find the training and support they need to develop their skills and talents in collaboration with other theatre practitioners. If this scheme fails, the failure of British Theatre to nourish new talent, and to find a way to be innovative and exciting into the year 2000 will become more apparent as we increasingly exchange theatrical productions with our European partners.

Cheryl is currently writing *The Taking of Liberty* for her M.A. in Playwriting at Birmingham University.

WORKSHOP WRITINGS

TIME AND PLACE

Sugar,
If you are passing in your car —
In the opposite direction
and you notice my silk black legs
        my provocative hips and
    the sunshine in my eyes, —
and the mood takes you to —
comment
on my loveliness —
of course I will flirt and wave
behaving like you are my only true love.
I will shoot kisses through the air
and share
this fleeting intimacy.
If
you are passing
In your car —
in the opposite
direction.

But —
If it's late.
If I have missed the last bus
and, in desperation
I am rabbit–darting home
If it's dark
and
cold
and there's a dampness in the air
and the ghosts of the day just passed
whisper warnings.
If you come driving by,
Aretha Franklin in your ears
protected by the
warmth and speed of —
your metal love
If you
see me
and opportunity springs to mind...

don't stop mister
just don't stop.

a–dziko Simba

DESIRE

Bubbles in Euston Station
Blown by a child
Rise up
And give a new dimension
To your smile.

They burst
And in the tiny drops
Of sparkling liquid
I see my feelings crystallise.

Later
Our train hurtles
Through the darkened Midlands
On and on
Northward bound.

We breast another express
And in its dimly lit corridor
I watch two lovers
Embrace with passion
A film–still
Suddenly becoming
You and I

Recognition
An electric shock
Shoots through me

I look at you
Sitting back quietly
Against the second class seat
And wonder if you know
That I am burning with desire
You do not
As I shall soon discover.

Anne Hazel Clare

THE EMPTY BEDROOM

Bared of your things
Our bedroom has become
A place of terror.
Your glowing rugs,
Your multi–coloured paperbacks
Are branded on my memory.

That blood stain
We covered with your kilim
Is back again.
It grins at me with yellowed teeth.
I look away,
But blank walls stare out at me
I stare back
At an agony of white emulsion...
Oh how shall I ever sleep here now?

I turn out the light
To switch off the pain,
But smirking in darkened corners,
Behind cupboard doors,
On the shadowy dressing–table
Lurks the carbon copy of your smile.

And then
Your ghost voice,
A B.B.C. archive recording,
Starts up in my reluctant brain.
It utters all your favourite phrases.
I block my ears.

But you natter on inside my head.
Aching with your absent presence
I clench my teeth
Take out a cigarette for relief
Only to find the ashtray full
Of your dead ends.

Late
Lurid under the electric glare
I snatch up some paper
And scribble senseless things.

Anne Hazel Clare

THE SNAKE

The snake slithers on the full–of–clothes floor
at times we can see it   at times we cannot
emerald green, ebony black, shiny smooth scales
It looks benevolent enough; but beware
it's a snake, let us be aware

Our room is crammed, although none too small
somewhere in a high–rise block   detached
I stand shivering   You curl mesmerised
fully trusting the creature and its promise
of sex unknown

The snake knows this   full of confidence
it advances, wraps its body around you
you in total surrender, in eager anticipation
its tongue, fast flickers, marks your neck
which you caress with ecstatic fondness

the snake retreats, withdraws
it now is harmless and very satisfied.

I hold my heart from jumping out; this bite may
be poison, killing you slowly within the hour
I have to find a doctor, someone who knows.
I have to. It might not be too late.
You might be saved still.

You oblivious, are in a trance
the pleasure that got sucked into you
is giving you all you want   you don't
mind if this kiss will cost your life
you never valued her much anyway

I must get out. I must run.
I am not as frightened as I should be
I wonder: Is there something I don't want to see?
That you'd rather die from pleasure given
than live in boredom given and taken?

Nina Rapi

LOVERS

As I curved round my lover's side,
Beach warm, gold dusted, wave smoothed,
I lost my body even as I found it.

Edges, skin, lines blurred,
And the dark that moulded us
Spun us away, unthreading sleeping flesh.

The night swallowed us whole,
Leaving an empty bed
And an open window.

In the honeyed dust that holds me,
My lover lies hidden,
Beyond my reach, beyond my eyes.

It is the dark that caresses me now.
Changing my shape as it brushes skin,
Claiming its own, fast and secret.

Polly Thomas

THE NEW MAN

He walks like a non–sexist man
Slightly hen–toed, lean.
He fixes his lightly–greased hair,
Looks confused, rather than mean.

Adjusting his fifties' jacket,
More loosely on his shoulder,
He wonders if he'll grow a beard
And donate sperm when he's older.

His jeans are ripped at the knee,
But don't show signs of wear,
He used to have a peace dove badge
To show how much he cared.

He sports two left–ear earrings,
Which make people think he's gay,
He likes to be ambiguous
But won't go all the way.

He never sticks his chest out
Nor swings his arms too high,
He's bold amongst his buddies,
But women find him shy.

He's had his consciousness raised
At least three times before,
He's careful not to interrupt
Unless he's keen to score.

His toilet manners are improving,
He always aims straight in,
He replaces the seat thoughtfully
And sometimes empties the bin.

He's always highly chivalrous
To women, opening doors,
But always fails to notice
The pregnant woman who's footsore,
As he sits on the crowded tube
Reading Heartland Ads —
He's searching for a feminist,
Who'll say he's not like other lads.

Cherry Smyth

"Maybe he's not who he said he was, and had to leave you before you found out. Maybe he's not a writer at all, but a poll tax collector, or a CIA agent, or even a Tory MP." suggested Sam rather wildly.

"Maybe."

"Whatever else, he's a jerk." pronounced Sam, pouring sweetened condensed milk over her bowl of bananas. This culinary delight was the only thing Katy could think of that could even slightly cheer her up. She had just been jilted by a gawky writer called Leonard whom she had met at a party several months earlier. They had spent four tempestuous months together and the end had come, according to Katy, just as they were beginning to fall in love with each other.

Samantha now applied herself seriously to the problem in hand.

"Is it definitely over, or will he start asking you back in a few days?"

"It's absolutely, utterly, completely and irrevocably over."

"Right. I get the picture." Sam scrutinised her friend with the professionalism of a trained draughtsman. "It can't be because you aren't attractive enough."

"Oh can't it? Can't it just? He may have been physically repulsed by me for all I know."

"Unlikely," said Sam with confidence. "What about sex?"

"Oh it was great. At least, I thought it was great. Maybe he hated it but couldn't bring himself to tell me, maybe..."

"Stop." commanded Sam. Katy stopped.

"Which of you made most of the running? I mean, which of you initiated sex most often?"

"Oh, me of course" replied Katy cheerfully, licking the sweetened condensed milk off her fingers with relish.

"You don't think I was too sexually demanding for him do you? My Mum always warned me against that — I thought she was just trying to stop me having fun."

"It's possible. Unlikely, but possible. Did he ever say anything to make you think it might be true?"

Katy stared intently at the chair opposite her. "Number One..." She began. Since girlhood Katy and Sam had always resorted to list–making in times of crisis.

"...when we were driving to Northumberland, Leonard was talking about Nietzsche, and just out of devilment, I said, 'Who's he?' 'Surely you've heard of Nietzsche?' he said. And just to spite him I never admitted I was joking. That really embarrassed him. Number Two: He was talking about some friends of his, a couple, and in his ranting voice he said, 'God, I can't stand it, she's got him round her little finger, chained to the sink of her petty, tedious little mind, doing endless washing–up in the emotionally dirty water of her horrid little psychoses.' Isn't that a weird thing to say? Then he gave me a crazed sort of stare and laughed maniacally."

"Katy, are you making this up?" questioned Sam sternly.

"Number Three," continued Katy unheeding. "Only a few days ago we were brushing our teeth looking at each other in the mirror and he suddenly stopped and gazed at me for a minute and said, 'God Katy, I almost love you!'"

"Perhaps he really was falling in love with you, but couldn't handle it?"

"Perhaps."

"Perhaps he thought you were too independent, and what he really wanted was a nice, reliable girlfriend to come home to every evening!"

"Perhaps he wanted me to chain him to the sink, and whip him with wooden spoons... This isn't really helping,"

"Well, have you talked it over with him?"

"I've tried."

"And?"

"He won't!"

"What does he say?"

"That there's nothing to say."

"Oh."

"I tried to get him drunk to make him talk."

"Good idea."

"He thought I was trying to seduce him ."

"Oh dear."

"I tried to make him have a row with me."

"And?"

"He told me he couldn't discuss it until we had both calmed down." Sam slumped defeated for a moment.

"Tell you what. Let's adjourn this and go out on the bike. I'll take you on a tour of all the bridges of London, West to East." Katy brightened visibly. "Even as far as Hammersmith?"

"Even as far as Hammersmith."

Leonard had been writing his first novel when he met Katy. As he explained to his friends, this lightness of hers, this propensity to be distracted by a new idea, to up and follow it without a backward glance, both captivated and maddened him. "Like a dragonfly among bullrushes," he said, feeling himself firmly cast as a bullrush. He never loved her more than the day, soon after they'd met, when over breakfast she coolly announced her intention to emigrate to Southern Spain, and become a potter. "I could grow old in London, doing boring jobs and freezing to death every winter. Why bother, when I could do boring jobs in the blazing heat and eat churros and chocolate every morning for breakfast?" and she shrugged her shoulders in a Mediterranean way, as if she was already there.

He enjoyed talking of her as a luminescent, airy creature who might disappear into the dawn at any moment. But he misunderstood Katy. She happily left places behind with no trace of regret, but rarely did she leave people. Instead, she swept them up and along with her in her glad eccentric flight. It was Leonard who left people behind. He allowed only places to anchor him. He was even loathe to go with her when she suggested a weekend together in Northumberland. He finally agreed, but delayed their departure for several hours with last–minute tasks. Katy sat on the floor and annoyed him by laughing at things in the paper and reading them out.

"Poor Leonard, you hate holidays, don't you?" she said when they finally arrived in Bamburgh.

"No." said Leonard, wishing he was back in his Brixton flat with his possessions neatly around him. His mood worsened with every hour that passed.

"You're doing your best to make this a disaster, aren't you?"

"No." said Leonard.

But after a protracted argument on the rain swept sands of Bamburgh Bay, Leonard said,

"Let's face it. We're fundamentally unsuited to each other. Wouldn't it be best for both of us if we just don't see each other any more?"

Katy was baffled. "But why? We have such fun together, sometimes. And we still could."

"No." said Leonard, "No, no NO!" For him the case was shut.

***

In time, Katy gave up trying to understand or explain what had happened. She even stopped trying to apportion blame rationally. Instead, she set her considerable creative abilities to devising a plan for revenge.

He wasn't allowing her a decent finale, with all the build–ups and wind–downs necessary. She really didn't want to just disappear into the dawn.

She realised she still had a key to Leonard's flat. She found it when she tipped the contents of her bag onto the floor of her bedroom, and systematically eliminated from the pile, every last bus ticket, restaurant bill and cashpoint receipt that reminded her of him. With the key in her hand, she succumbed to a dizzying sense of power.

One morning, she rang the magazine where Leonard worked to check he was there and then went to his flat and let herself in. His home was small and barren and perfectly neat. The floors were bare boards with black paint slapped over them. In the kitchen were two plates, two mugs, two eggs and a pint of milk. In the sitting–room was one dralon–covered armchair, a stack music system, a colour television with video and a compact disc player, which had arrived since Katy's departure. The walls were covered with shelves of books, alphabetically arranged in order of author.

His expensive 531 frame racing–bike with Campagnolo fittings was kept locked in the bedroom alongside the single mattress on the floor, a cupboard containing clean white Y–fronts and an Amstrad PCW 8256 on a desk by the window. Katy stood in the bedroom, hands on hips, surveying the scene and then she went into the kitchen to make herself a cup of tea.

While the kettle was boiling, she looked through the compact discs and put on her favourite Bach cello suite. She felt like a peeping tom, and the sensation was liberating. She ran herself a hot bath and lay in it for forty minutes. She got out feeling refreshed and carefully cleaned away the ring. She walked into Leonard's room wearing Leonard's towel and got into Leonard's bed. The smell reminded her of him, and his slender fingers. For a moment she thought she might cry but instead she masturbated. It seemed a more positive vent for her feelings.

Sitting at the desk, she noticed all Leonard's discs containing his Great English Novel. On one set of discs was written "Final Version. Print and send to RM by Sept. 16." Katy stared at the discs — it was the twelfth of September today. She took a sheet of typing paper and wrote a list:

1. Insert disc into PCW 8256 and switch off at mains.
2. Pass big magnet over disc.
3. Submerge disc in hot water.
4. Store disc in freezer
5. Put disc under grill
6. Break open disc with sledgehammer.

But she was too curious to destroy them without first having looked at them so she switched on the Amstrad and settled down to read the Great English Novel.

She didn't really expect to find herself the heroine but what did astonish her was the extent to which she was absent from it. It was a chronicle of Leonard's life — the urban intellectual in post–Thatcherite Britain. The men in the story took a lot of drugs and sat up all night in South London squats discussing art and politics — and drugs. The women were terrifyingly beautiful and unpredictable. They never showed signs of sexual jealousy and didn't seem concerned about contraception. The men were so worried about A.I.D.S. they never went anywhere without being armed to the teeth with condoms. Katy thought this particularly ironic.

By the time she had finished reading, she felt as if small, dislocated parts of her had been scattered throughout the book. She spotted her over–wide mouth on page twelve, her inability to remember telephone numbers on page fifty–four, her hatred of Doberman Pinschers on page seventy–three, her red silk hat on page one hundred–and–one, her chronic unpunctuality on page one hundred–and–ten and on page one hundred–and–forty–six, a particularly embarrassing thing, she once cried out while having sex with Leonard.

He hadn't mentioned how she had helped him with his tax claim, or how she had showed him how to park a car. He hadn't even included her fine, strong swimmer's arms.

Katy sat in the chair and frowned, resting her chin on her fist in an attitude of intense concentration. The flat was very still and silent. The only sound came from the Amstrad which flickered greenly and made small buzzing noises. Outside in the road, sirens screamed in convoys on their way to the prison, a helicopter circled overhead, and a hundred different aeroplanes set off for far away destinations. But Katy remained intent on the screen.

She looked at the discs fixedly. Then an idea slipped into her head, like a late–comer finding her seat after the concert has started. A slow smile spread across Katy's over–wide mouth.

She put the first disc back into the machine and called up a page early in the book where the hero and his Alter Ego are discussing at length, the supremacy of 'Form' over 'Content' in 'Art.' At the end of the scene Katy typed in a tiny insert which read, "The Woman came in wearing her Red Silk Hat. She said to him, 'Hey, here's the athlete's foot powder you wanted.'"

She giggled aloud and looked guiltily round and then carried on scanning the text. A few pages later she spotted one of the characters telling Katy's best joke. After the punchline, she inserted, "Nobody laughed. After a moment Diego said, 'Its the way you tell them. They just aren't as funny as when the Woman in the Red Hat tells them.'"

Now she was really enjoying herself. She went to the page where the Leonard character stays up all night having a sexuality crisis because he thinks he's fallen in love with a very rich and reactionary Fleet Street Reporter, he meets in a late–night cafe in Smithfield Market. As day breaks he returns to his untidy flat and turns on the telephone answering machine. Into this scene Katy added an extra phone message, from the Hero's mother: "Hello darling, Mum here. Just ringing to see how you are. Could you let me have that honeysuckle print duvet cover back quite soon — Aunty Elsie needs it. Lots of love. Bye."

Next, emboldened by her success, Katy tackled the sex scene. In Leonard's version it was effortless, immaculate and climaxes with Katy's embarrassing cry. Katy set to work erasing the word 'girl' and replacing it with 'woman' then she swapped round the text so that Leonard is the one who utters the embarrassing cry. Finally, she gave the woman a few extra lines such as, "What do you mean, you won't use a condom?" and "No, not like that, try this" and finally "Don't stop NOW!"

Katy was chortling with pleasure as she combed through the text, meticulous as a forensic scientist, liberally scattering partisan remarks among the characters such as, "Ask the Woman with the Red Silk Hat. She knows everything there is to know about computers." and later, "I think I've behaved very badly to my girlfriend. I'm an insensitive shit." and her piece de resistance, in the mouth of the Leonard character, "I've read Nietzsche time and again but it was only when the Woman with the Red Hat explained it to me that I began to understand anything at all."

With that, Katy wiped her fingerprints off the discs and put them carefully back where she'd found them. She rearranged the bedding exactly as it had been, hung up the towel where she'd found it, washed up her mug and replaced the compact disc in its rightful place. With one final glance round the flat, she let herself out and took a bus down to the river. Feeling euphoric and wicked, still laughing aloud as she walked, she went to the Albert Bridge. Rush hour commuters sat bumper to bumper on the bridge, but ignoring them all, she walked purposefully to the middle and with all her strength hurled the key to Leonard's flat into the sallow depths of the Thames.

* * * *

Six months later, Katy was in Spain. She had talked her way into a job apprenticed to a famous ceramicist, a woman with strong, brown hands and clay in her cuticles. She allowed Katy to use all the facilities and sell her own work in the studio shop. One morning, sitting at a pavement cafe drinking Spanish brandy she had in front of her a letter from Sam and a two–day old copy of 'The Independent.' When she'd finished chuckling over the letter she opened the newspaper and discovered a review of Leonard's book:

> A potentially turgid first novel, just saved by the strong but elusive presence of "the Woman in the Red Silk Hat" who never fails to debunk, demystify and deconstruct the self–conscious prose of the main character. An interesting narrative experiment and unusual to find such sensitivity and self–mockery in a young man's writing — disappointing therefore, that he is suddenly, inexplicably unavailable for interview.

Beside the review there was a photograph of Leonard looking lean. Katy smiled at the waiter when he came with her bill, and sat doodling idly while she waited for her change. When the waiter came back she found she had drawn a woman's silk hat on the photo of Leonard. She and the waiter laughed at the doodle, then she walked off into the city leaving it lying on the table.

Clare Bayley

71

BABY BABY

Oh baby, you're sooo sweet.
Oh baby, you're sooo fine.
Open those blue eyes wider, baby,
And promise to be mine.

See baby's big round eyes
Gaze innocently out.
Your skin's as soft as peaches, baby,
And that's what love's about.

But baby — you know I love you true –
So let me whisper in your ear,
As I stroke your rounded thigh,
You're just a little too fat — here!

Yes baby, you're mine for ever more,
I'll love you 'til I die –
But those rolls on rolls of baby's fat –
Oh baby, don't start to cry!

I'm only speaking as a man –
It's truly what I feel –
I want you to be my loving baby.
But that's the last time I buy you a meal!

Come on baby, don't shout like that!
You're just too fat to be a lady.
And I only want to be proud of you –
Hey! There's no need to go crazy!

Well. I'm shocked at your response!
If you can't, won't get trim,
I'm off and out the door –
To find a real woman — thin!

Polly Thomas

DAVID SAID

David said to me
"Writing poems is like
Being sick on the page."
I said
"There's a poem in that."
And wished I'd said it myself.
David said that feminism
was a conspiracy to divide the working class
(And almost forgot to add
That he admired the miners' wives)
But I was washing up
And couldn't quite hear.
David said
"Living in London is a
Statement.
Confronting life."
I wondered if I'd missed the last tube,
And waited for a break
In the conversation.
David said
"You're paranoid about all this
Rape and stuff.
I've lived in Deptford all my life."
David said
He wished I'd talk to him
Like he talked to me
As I turned the gas on
He missed the intellectual
Stimulus
As I let the gas collect
The cut and thrust
As he picked up a Marlboro
Of male debate
But I just smiled
And handed him his Zippo
As I waved goodbye

David always said he wanted to go with a bang.

Janet Beck

73

POLLO

It was October, I was in the Pollo bar, and the nights had started to get dark early. Even though it was only seven o'clock, the blackness seemed to be thick in the restaurant. Everyone was wearing black except for me — I was wearing grey (I always knew I was different). I felt an oppressive buzzing, it was constricting my body.

In the Pollo bar students from St. Martin's School of Art gathered. I didn't want to meet Robert here, but he said it was the only restaurant he knew. Two people were at the table in front of me listening to a big American bloke, talking about his thesis in a loud voice, all about a trendy American film director. Showing off just by mentioning the name, getting off on the association — I notice he doesn't say what he actually wrote. (And anyone can go round saying "Martin Scorcese, Robert De Niro, Woody Allen..." but does it make them interesting?)

He's talking to this girl he obviously fancies. (These people are talking about films when all they want is sex.) The girl with black hair, black eyeliner, black jumper, black mini–skirt, black tights, black shoes and a black coat is looking very attentive. He's trying to impress her. The only trouble is that her boyfriend has his arm round her and is gently carressing her forearm and waist. She gets up to go, but the boyfriend holds on and keeps stroking her arm, while the big man talks American film directors. The girl is obviously lapping it all up. (Monkeys, take me to the ape house.)

The waitress, Italian or Polish, stinking mood, asks me what I want. I explain that I'm waiting for a friend. She gives me the obligatory dirty look and goes. I try to look as though I'm waiting for an incredibly handsome guy to arrive, even though I know it's only Robert. Some people would say he was handsome, but I know what's behind the bright blue eyes, the thin skin and the thick brown hair slicked up and back.

In he walks smiling. I want to slap his face. That girl's looking at him — good, now she's looking at me. I give a superior smile. (I've got him, you haven't, fuck off.)

"Where have you been? I hate waiting for people. We should've arranged to meet outside."

"Then we mightn't have got a table." Robert looks around, notices all the young women, makes me feel superfluous.

"Have you finished looking?"

"Yes, have you finished moaning?"

But, he looks around again, and smiles at that cow in black. (Hasn't she gone yet?)

The waitress plonks herself in front of us. "Would you like to order?"

"We'll just look at the menu." Robert says. She sighs and goes away.

"It's all in Italian. I don't know what half of it is."

"Just order something. Anything."

74

He clicks his fingers at the waitress. (He even clicks his fingers in Pizza Hut.) She comes up.

"I'll have this Riggatoni with this sauce."

"What sauce is that?" I said pointing at the Italian writing on the menu.

"I think it's mushroom and something." Says Robert.

The waitress shuffles around to look.

"What's this please ?"

"Spaghetti and clam and tomato and garlic sauce."

"And this?"

Very long drawn out sigh. "Garlic, spinach, pepper, and cream cheese."

"Green pepper? Red pepper? Black...."

"For God's sake Carmel, will you order instead of asking what colour the fucking pepper is?"

"I'll have that." I said, pointing at the menu without looking at it.

"I wish I hadn't asked you out tonight."

"So do I. Thanks a lot for psyching me up for an enjoyable evening. I wish I was somewhere else. I wish I was on holiday on a Greek Island with..."

"I wish I was fucking that girl over there."

"I wish I was that girl over there, because you'd never get anywhere near me."

Then Robert's friend Tim arrived. I often thought about going out with Robert's friend Tim. I've never told Robert I fancy Tim. He suspects, but I always deny it.

"Hiya, Tim, Robert never said you were coming."

"I forgot to mention it, you were so busy telling me what you want."

"What do you want Carmel?" (Tim's ten times nicer than Robert. Why doesn't he fancy me? He hasn't even got a girlfriend.)

"She wants someone to buy her expensive foreign holidays."

"No, I don't. I want a man who's loving and affectionate — who cares for me."

"You'll never get anyone like that." Robert was definite on this.

Tim didn't want to order. Our food came. I couldn't remember what I ordered, but I knew it wasn't what I got. It had no taste. The pasta was dry, the sauce was peppery and I wanted to get out.

We walked out of the restaurant into Old Compton Street. Tim invited us to a party at his mate's house. Then, when we passed a wine shop, he wanted to get a bottle so we all went in and bought a bottle each. Tim said he'd carry mine so I stood outside the shop, waiting. I fiddled with my purse, checking my money and my Travelcard and whether I'd got my front door key. Tim and Robert came out with the wine and I began to feel happier. We were going out to a party and we all liked each other for the night.

We turned to go when a scruffy kid came dashing past and grabbed my purse. Everything I owned in my blood red purse. All my bits of paper, lists of shopping, phone numbers I hadn't put in my diary, a few pounds, my credit cards and a peppermint tea bag.

I was still for half a second and then I ran. Robert was calling out "No, Carmel, it might be dangerous," but I ran on, faster than any sprinter, dodging people like a cheetah, leaving Robert's words to fall into empty space. I caught up with the boy well into Wardour Street, yanked his arm back, took the purse and then pushed his face and body up against a wall as hard as I could.

He was about fifteen years old but lighter than I expected and when he tried to scramble away, I pushed him down on to the pavement. Then Robert and Tim caught up and the boy tried even harder to run away so I kicked him in the groin, held his arm again and pushed his face right up against the wall. His nose and mouth were bloody now and he started to yelp like a puppy.

"Don't move, or I'll break your arm right off. We're going to find a policeman."

"Don't do that, you've done enough to him." Tim said.

"Let him go," said Robert.

"Fuck off. Go and find a policeman, will you?" I shouted. The boy who was terrified, seemed to gain confidence once he realised my friends weren't backing me up. I yanked his arm so far up his back, that I felt the joint give. He screamed. A couple of people stopped in the street to watch. Robert and Tim stared at me like I was the criminal.

I stood a few inches away from the boy then let go and kicked him in the back. He went face first into the pavement, and then scrambled off. There was blood running down my hand. I was panting and sweating. I had so much energy inside me I could've run after him again and carried on beating him, but once he was gone, I felt that first surge of anger leave me.

I turned to Robert, his mouth was hanging open. I could see that he couldn't understand, had never done an impulsive act in his putrid existence, could never let civilisation peel off him, would never feel twenty-seven years of anger rise up.

"He won't be doing that again in a hurry..." They stared at me unable to believe what they'd seen.

"I got it back." I said, holding my red purse up for everyone to see.

"How could you do that? I've never seen violence like that."

"You haven't seen much then, have you?"

"You were just out to get him."

"I wanted my purse back. What was I supposed to do, ask him for it? It didn't look as though you were going to help me."

"I wouldn't help you, after what you've done."

"He stole my purse. Was I supposed to wait for it to fall back into my hands?"

"It was only a material thing." Now Tim was chiming in too.

"Only! It was my bloody purse. It belonged to me."

"He looked as though he didn't have any...." ('Money'– he left off. The redistribution of wealth...Robin Hood and his merry men.)

"You could've broken his arm." said Robert.

"I'm sorry I didn't."

"You're as bad as him." (Tim had quite a bad case of social conscience.)

"I don't like violence." Robert said.

"I don't like violence." I said.

"I don't like revenge." Tim said.

"I believe in rubbing a dog's nose in the shit immediately after the event, so they know exactly what it's about."

"You were enjoying it." Robert was really playing superior now, closely backed up by Tim. "You're a sadist Carmel."

"And you're both voyeurs."

Maybe my evening wasn't ruined after all. Because I looked at these two apologies for men, looked at their excuses for action, looked at their hostility towards me and I knew I was free of Robert and Tim and going out for boring evenings full of petty arguments forever.

I walked away.

Alison Prager

MANY HANDS

These are the hands
that push and pull
push and pull

Push their way to work
on buses and tubes
in the rush–crush hour

Remembering the hungry eyes
These are the hands
that rub each other
in incestuous pain
and bury deep
in tattered pockets
to keep from feeling cold

Finding their way to offices
They press buttons and
sweep brooms and
slap the boss man's facety face

Always remembering the hungry eyes

With corns and cuts and
blisters and bumps
that wipe and wash
the windows and walls
upon the thirteenth floor

These are the digits of dirt

Flexing and bending
bending and bracing
lifting boxes and
tables and
chairs

Remembering the hungry eyes

These are the fingers that
flick through the pay packet
knowing soon
they will pick and poke
through trays of fruit
and vegetables

Remembering the hungry eyes

These are the fingers that
flick through the packet
and bang on the desk of
the man in the office
on floor thirteen
because they remember
the hungry eyes
all in a row
that wait for the food
chopped and cooked
by these very same hands.

These are the hands
that push and pull,
push and pull

These are the hands
that realise

The money
is never
enough.

a–dziko Simba

SAN GIORGIO MAGGIORE

Sun soaks into hot marble,
Only Palladio's dome offers refuge
From the glare; inside all is still,
Footsteps swallowed in the emptiness.
Outside the chequered slabs are empty.

Across the few yards of choppy water
Sunlight fights to find a space between the feet
Of the thousands who crowd the square,
Following the tradition of a thousand years.

In the palace or on the island,
Away from the crowds
The decisions are made,
As they have been for a thousand years.

Jean Abbott

THE GONDOLIER'S WIFE

What do you do all day
While your husband struts the streets
Or stands poised and balanced
Above the dark green water?
The oar transfers the power of his mind and body
Into the boat's smooth progress
Through impossibly narrow channels
Collision–free.
Who presses his immaculate trousers?
Do you spend your days in some dark kitchen
Washing his crisp white shirts by hand,
While he, the master of water,
Flirts with foreign girls
As he touts for trade?
Does he smile and laugh with you
At midnight when he returns?
Or has it been a good day for trade
And the long hours of rhythmic sway
Send him straight down into sleep?
Do you watch your neighbour's regular hours,
And envy his wife her certainty and steady wage?
Do you share your husband's pride,
Love him for his skill,
Basking in his reflected glory?
Or do you long to be free
Of the shuttered room and shady square
And sparkle with him, like him
In the world of sunlight and water?

Jean Abbott

PAST THE PASTA

When he came back it was very late and I asked him where he'd been, but I kept my voice light, sing–song, so he wouldn't put his guard up. It worked.

"Circumstances beyond my control I'm afraid, silly".

It occurred to me, for the first time, how much I hated this pet name he'd given me.

"This last minute run came in and there was no–one else that could do it".

Well, I knew that was a lie, like I knew all the other times were lies. Only this time he wasn't going to talk his way out of it, because it wasn't just intuition. This time I had what they call corroborative evidence. I'd spoken to their telephonist, Angie. Nice girl, but bored. Boring job. So I always make a point of having a little chat with her. We're on first name terms now. Anyway, I waited until just before six and I phoned and said I was sorry to ring at the last minute, but I'd just remembered something important I had to ask Nick. Had I rung in time to catch him? "Oh Silvia", she said, "I am sorry. You've just missed him. He left at quarter to. He should be home any time now."

He should be home any time now. That's more or less what I've been saying to myself, every other night for weeks. Funny how a single sentence can get stuck in your head and go round and round. I do it with songs all the time. The other night I got Top Gun out on video, just to pass the time. There's a bit in that where Tom Cruise sings 'You've lost that loving feeling' to Kelly McGillis in this bar. Well that stuck with me for days. Nearly drove me nuts. I used to have the radio on all the time, but lately it just gets on my nerves. I prefer silence.

I've been down and joined the library, but I haven't really got into any of the books yet and they're nearly due back. Just can't concentrate on anything at the moment. Before Nick and I met I was like a bookworm. That's what ruined my eyesight, according to my dad. "Pity," he said, "a young girl like you, having to wear glasses." I suppose I could get contacts. They're a bit pricey though and like Nick says,

"… if you're buying your own home you have to be prepared to make sacrifices."

That's why he's been doing all this overtime, I expect. Ha. Ha.

I wonder if he's done any overtime at all. It's not as if I've ever gone on at him for more money, but then I suppose he's had some extra expenses recently. If there's one thing I'm good at, it's managing the finances. I usually walk the long way from the bus stop so I can go by the greengrocers and the local butcher. There is a supermarket the other way but it works out more expensive and the stuff's never as good. You know what they say about the way to a man's heart. The girls at work think I'm mad. They all dash out at lunchtime to Marks and Spencer to get their pre–prepared meals and bugger the expense. Excuse my language. Nice

82

stuff, though. Sometimes I even sneak a look at the side of the boxes to get inspiration.

The other day I did red cabbage and apple, baked potato with sour cream and chives and pork chops cooked in juniper berries. It smelt wonderful. I was starving. I thought, "Well, he should be home any time now".....Half an hour later the pork chops were beginning to curl up at the edges and the red cabbage was looking pretty sad, so I turned the whole lot off. I suppose I could have eaten it on my own, but I'd lost my appetite somehow. Nick ate some when he finally got back, but he only picked at it. I don't think he felt like eating. Well you don't really, do you? Not at that time of night. Not when you've just had to do a 'last minute run'.

So, since that little episode I've been racking my brains to think of stuff that won't spoil. Tonight I made spaghetti, so when I heard the car pull up I put the biggest pan on to boil.

When he said that, about having to do a last minute run, that was the moment when I finally had to accept it. Although really I knew when I saw the cigarette ends in the car ash–tray. Dunhill have gold rings around the filters, my Silk Cut don't. So, it was just confirmation really. I didn't say anything. Salted the water and watched the first little bubbles come up around the edges. It wasn't for the pasta, you see, it was meant for him. The whole lot, straight in the face. His beautiful face. I don't know why I even got the spaghetti out of the jar. Automatic pilot I suppose.

Nick came up behind me, just as it came to the boil and kissed the top of my head and said how good it smelt and how he loved my cooking. He was as close to me as you are now. If I'd just grabbed the handle and wheeled round, it would have been so easy.

I didn't though. I took the spaghetti in my right hand and stuck it in the pan. My hand, I mean.

Mary Aspinwall.

83

SISTAS' ALMS (RELIEF)

....and when she'd said
"please"
more times than pride allowed and
heard enough
"nos"
to fill the world
when she launched herself from
social security's 10th floor
knowing that it was the only way she'd fly
....in this reality –

the women knew
but the men didn't understand

....and when she finally left
left him
left the children, the plants and
all those things
she'd carefully sewn together and
all she carried out was a suitcase
full of hope and
a pocket
full of pain –

the women knew
but the men didn't understand

....and when she rang to say
that
she wasn't coming back
that
she found more comfort in her sistas' arms

the women knew
but the men didn't understand.

....and when
fearing for her very life
she submitted
silently
never letting
RAPE
scream from her lips

the women knew
but the men didn't understand

....and that time she,
singing and crying
stripped to her naked self
on top of the 29 home
believing that
she was the second coming –

the women knew
but the men didn't understand

....and when she let go
                    or aborted
                    or gave her children away
                    or smothered them with her love
                    or pushed them far with her fear
                    or prayed each night by their beds
not to live the life she had

the women knew.

                                        a–dziko Simba.

MIDNIGHT FEAST

The two girls had never met before. They were thrown together that evening by Sid's parents coming to visit Elizabeth's and stopping the night. The two mothers had been at school together. It was a re–union for them, a first meeting for the girls.

Elizabeth was thirteen and already at secondary school. Sid was eight, still a "little girl," as Elizabeth informed her early in the evening. The parents went out soon after their arrival to make an evening of it.

The babysitter, an elderly woman who was devoted to her knitting, was sitting downstairs in front of the television. She had been babysitting for Elizabeth for some years now. Elizabeth seemed to have her well in control and told Sid that she would not move from the armchair except to make herself a pot of tea.

Elizabeth's mum had shown Sid where she was to sleep — in Elizabeth's room. She was excited to be sharing a room with another girl. She was an only child. Maybe they would have a midnight feast. When she stayed with a school friend, they'd had one.

Sid's mum told Elizabeth and the babysitter to make sure Sid was in bed by seven–thirty. Until then, Sid played quietly with some of Elizabeth's games while Elizabeth got on with her homework, conveying to Sid an air of mystery and importance about the work. Sid would have like to have watched the television — her parents didn't have one — but Elizabeth told her that too much television wasn't good for her and that she should play instead.

Sid liked the look of the babysitter. She was plump and kindly–looking — the sort you could cuddle up to — like her grandma. Sid assumed the babysitter would see her off to bed, but Elizabeth took charge and sent her off to bed, not a second later than half–past seven. Sid was a little disappointed not to have a few extra minutes (her babysitter always allowed this) but Elizabeth was very firm.

Sid went up to Elizabeth's room obediently. She looked at some of the pictures on the walls — lurid, glossy magazine cut–outs of pop–stars. She was excited to see an older girl's room, but also a little bit in awe and she felt as though she were intruding on someone else's private world. The animals on the chair surprised her — she'd thought Elizabeth was too big for such things.

She undressed, got into her pyjamas, went to the toilet and then snuggled down in the little bed in the corner. She felt wide awake. It was a cool evening in late spring. It wasn't dark yet and she could hear birds singing on the trees in the street outside.

Elizabeth came into the room. She went over to Sid's bed. Sid looked up at her, eyes wide open and smiling. Elizabeth frowned: "Aren't you asleep yet?"

"No, I feel wide awake," she said, feeling that this might be a game in which she was the little girl and Elizabeth her mother. Elizabeth sat on the bed and sternly announced she would count to fifty and by then Sid must be asleep — "...or else." Sid turned on her side towards Elizabeth, still feeling excited and shut her eyes tight trying to feel sleepy. She began to feel a little anxious because she still felt so wide awake and Elizabeth seemed serious about her going to sleep quickly. Sid tried to count herself, but the numbers kept colliding with the image of a stern–faced Elizabeth sitting over her and she lost count.

Sid opened one eye a fraction and saw Elizabeth seated on the bed, glaring at her. She snapped her eye shut, but Elizabeth had spotted it.

"You're not asleep," she said in an annoyed tone. "You naughty little girl. I'll give you one last chance to go to sleep. This time I'll count to one hundred. If you're not asleep by then, I'll have to punish you."

"Can I just go to the toilet?" asked Sid, suddenly feeling the urge to pee. Maybe that was stopping her falling asleep.

"What do you say?" said Elizabeth fiercely.

"Please."

"That's better. Alright, I'm being very patient. I've got a lot more work to do. Hurry up."

Sid jumped out of bed and ran along to the toilet, feeling Elizabeth's glare follow her as she left the room. By now she was worried. It didn't seem like a game at all. Elizabeth had to get on with her work and she was holding her up.

She felt safe in the toilet, but knew she had to come out and face Elizabeth again. Suppose she couldn't go to sleep when she got back into bed? What would Elizabeth do? She sat on the toilet, but the pee wouldn't come. She strained — no pee. Then she heard steps and knew Elizabeth was standing outside the toilet door. She willed the pee out — but in it stayed. Finally, she squeezed out a few drops and wiped herself.

"What's taking you so long in there?" Elizabeth's voice hissed through the door. "Come out this minute."

Sid obeyed and felt a sharp smack on her bottom as she fled down the corridor and into bed. Elizabeth followed her and sat on the bed.

"Now I'll count to a hundred — and you'd better go to sleep," she said threateningly.

Sid wished Elizabeth would go downstairs and leave her alone. It was very hard to go to sleep feeling Elizabeth's bum against her legs, hemming her in. She turned over and tried to forget Elizabeth was there, but she couldn't. As the seconds passed and she knew Elizabeth must be nearing a hundred, she felt her body become rigid with waiting.

"One hundred" said Elizabeth with triumph. "And you're not asleep are you? It's no good pretending, I know you're not."

Sid turned and opened her eyes to meet a cold, accusing stare.

"I'm sorry, Elizabeth. I'm trying, really I am. I just feel awake."

She suddenly felt very small and very stupid for not being able to go to sleep.

"You're not trying hard enough. And you're wasting my time. I shall go downstairs now for half an hour to do my work. If you're not asleep when

87

I come back there really will be trouble." With this, Elizabeth swept out of the room and and slammed the door behind her.

Sid felt a huge relief — as if someone had just lifted a great weight off her. She stretched out in the bed, thankful Elizabeth was gone. Now she had a chance to go to sleep. It was hard to go to sleep to order, but Elizabeth didn't seem to understand this. Why was she being like this? Sid supposed it was her fault — she was being a nuisance, she was in the way. Perhaps Elizabeth didn't like someone else being in her room.

Once the initial relief wore off, Sid began to feel worried all over again. She only had half an hour. Half-an-hour. Perhaps Elizabeth would forget to come up again? She didn't think so. Elizabeth would be back. Would she be asleep by then? What if she wasn't? Elizabeth seemed to get angry with her very easily.

She felt more awake than ever. Her whole body was tense, waiting, listening, fearing. She wished her mother was there. She wished the babysitter would come up — instead of Elizabeth. She tossed and turned. Sleep avoided her. She went to the toilet again, worried she might wet the bed even though it was years since she had done that.

Back in bed, she heard footsteps on the stairs. Nerves gripped her. Was the half hour over already? It only seemed a few minutes since Elizabeth had left.

"Did you get out of bed?" asked Elizabeth accusingly, standing in the doorway.

"I had to go to the toilet."

"Again? You've only just been. You can't possibly have needed to go. You're lying. You've been snooping round my room."

"I haven't, I haven't. I just went to the toilet."

"You're to stay in bed! You're not to move from there unless I tell you. Understand? Now, go to sleep."

This time, Elizabeth left the door wide open. Sid heard her going back downstairs. She could hear sounds from the television. She didn't know what time it was, how much of the half-hour had gone and when Elizabeth would be up again. She felt shaky, upset and near to tears. If only she could please Elizabeth — by going to sleep. It was the one thing Elizabeth wanted her to do, the one thing she couldn't do. She must try harder. Her head felt as if it would burst with the effort of trying. She didn't feel sleepy for a second.

Once again, Sid heard steps on the stairs. She became tense with apprehension. But the steps passed her door and went on to the toilet. A few minutes later she heard the toilet flushing and the steps returning downstairs. Was it Elizabeth or the babysitter? She wanted to know. She tiptoed across the room, out of the door and to the head of the stairs in time to see the babysitter's figure disappearing into the living room. She wanted to call out to her — but what would she say? Somehow she knew it would make Elizabeth even angrier with her. She crept back to bed, feeling guilty for disobeying Elizabeth's order. Now she really had done something naughty.

More steps on the stairs. She knew it was Elizabeth this time. She turned to face the wall and shut her eyes. She heard the light switch turn on, felt the flood of light bearing down on her tightly closed eyes. She heard Elizabeth close the door behind her. She lay quite still, not daring to move. She heard rustling movements and a drawer being pulled in and out. Then two soft thuds — Elizabeth's shoes? Then she knew Elizabeth was standing by her bed, staring down at her.

"I know you're not asleep." The stern judgement cut through the silence. "You're not breathing properly."

Sid tried to breathe "properly." How did you breathe when you were asleep? It seemed an impossible thing to do.

"Stop pretending," snapped Elizabeth. "You're a naughty deceitful little girl. I shall have to tell your parents."

Sid gave up and opened her eyes to see Elizabeth standing beside the bed in a pink, knee–length nightie.

"Oh I'm sorry, Elizabeth, I am. I really did go to the toilet again and I am trying to go to sleep."

"You're not in the least bit sorry. You're not trying. You've decided to play–up tonight — just because your parents are out and you're in my room. Well you're not going to get away with it. I've given you every chance to behave and do what I tell you. Now I'm going to have to punish you."

Sid started to cry. She felt tired and frightened. She wished it would all end.

"Don't think you can get out of it by snivelling. Get out of bed."

Sid climbed out of bed sheepishly and stood awkwardly beside the bed.

"Stand here," commanded Elizabeth, pointing to a clear patch of floor in the middle of the room. "You're to stand there until I tell you you can move." Elizabeth climbed into her own bed and picked up a book from the bedside table.

Sid stood in the middle of the floor, watching Elizabeth, calmly reading in the comfort of her bed. Her feet were bare and the floor was chill. She felt an itch on the lower part of her leg and lifted her foot to rub it.

"Stop fidgeting!" Elizabeth ordered at once. "I told you you're not to move at all unless I say."

Sid quickly put her foot back on the floor. Elizabeth didn't seem to miss anything. She stood there for some time, thinking longingly of her bed and being able to lie down. Every time she lifted her feet even a tiny bit, Elizabeth snapped at her to keep still, but she found it impossible to stand completely motionless for very long. She knew Elizabeth was becoming more and more annoyed at her, but she could do nothing to stop it.

"Please can I get back in to bed and try to sleep?"

Elizabeth snapped her book shut with an ominous decisiveness. "It's impossible to read with you fidgeting and interrupting me. You just won't do what I tell you. You're a disobedient, wilful little girl. I can see there's nothing else for it — you'll have to learn the hard way." She got out of bed and came over towards Sid.

89

"Kneel down," she said.

Sid knelt, wishing Elizabeth would just let her go back to bed.

"No. Not like that. Your toes and feet are not to touch the ground. If they do, there'll be trouble."

Sid lifted her toes from the ground and nearly toppled over. Elizabeth caught her roughly and pushed her upright again.

"Stop messing about you little nuisance."

"I'm not — I'm trying, it's hard to do it."

"And don't make excuses. You're to kneel there like that for as long as I decide, understand?"

"Yes, Elizabeth," muttered Sid, choking back a sob that was rising in her throat.

"I'll be watching," threatened Elizabeth as she returned to her bed and sat on it, leaning against the headboard and staring at Sid. Sid looked down at the floor to avoid the unrelenting stare. Her whole body was trembling with the effort of balancing on her knees alone. She didn't know how long it'd be before she let her toes touch the floor, how long it'd be before she'd just fall over. She felt so tired. The desire to cry lessened as she concentrated on the act of balance required of her. If only she could do what Elizabeth wanted her to do, then Elizabeth might be satisfied and let her go to sleep. She thought of the bed in the corner, waiting for her. When would she be allowed to get into it again? It was very near to her — yet the distance between the bed and her seemed huge. The room took on giant proportions — all the objects in it seemed hazy and insubstantial, a mirage when set against the vast desert of the floor on which she felt marooned and pinioned by Elizabeth's will. She felt powerless to challenge Elizabeth. She imagined herself walking over the floor, into bed, but... She was terrified of what Elizabeth would do if she just got up and went to her bed, defied her like that. Her mother wasn't home yet. There was no one else who could help her.

Sid felt her feet moving down, down, towards the floor, dragged by some heavy weight. Her toes touched the floor and a relief flooded through her. She prayed Elizabeth would not notice.

"Didn't I tell you your feet were not to touch the floor?"

Quick as a flash, Sid lifted her toes again, feeling shooting pains in her legs; this alternated with a numbness of feeling which made it difficult to be sure whether her toes were off the floor or on it. She kept thinking she could feel the floor and trying to lift her feet further from it. She didn't know how long this lasted; it seemed hours in which she strained to carry out Elizabeth's orders and waited in dread for the fierce voice which would tell her she had failed.

"They're touching again! You little rat, I'm at my wit's end to know what to do with you. You are the most impossible child I've ever come across. Stand up."

Sid stood up shakily, feeling pins and needles in her legs and an ache in the lower part of her back. Her knees felt sore. Elizabeth came towards her.

"Take down your pyjama bottoms," she ordered.

Sid stared at her, thinking she hadn't heard right. Elizabeth repeated the instruction.

"Oh please Elizabeth let me go to bed. I'll go to sleep very quickly this time. I promise."

"Too late now. Take off your pyjama trousers this minute." Sid slowly pulled down the trousers and took them off, wishing her pyjama top was longer. She tried to pull it down to cover herself, but Elizabeth stopped her.

"Stay still! Let's have a look at what we have here." Her tone was sneering as she bent down and peered at Sid's private parts. "Turn round," she shoved and Sid felt her staring at her bottom. Elizabeth pulled her back round to face her and Sid immediately covered her crotch with her hands.

"Keep your hands by your side. You've nothing to hide. You're not a woman yet — you're just a little girl. Doesn't your father see you naked? One day you'll have lots of hair — all bushy — here," she tweaked at Sid's skin, "and blood will come out of here — and babies too."

She placed her hand between Sid's legs and roughly pushed it up against her. Sid thought she might be wet there.

Elizabeth abruptly took her hand away. "Ugh," she said. "You feel horrible there — that's because you're a bad little girl."

Sid began to shake with sobs and tears rolled down her face. She tried to keep the sobs small and quiet but she couldn't.

"You're such a sniveller — you baby. Because you've been bad, you'll have to be spanked. Crying won't help you."

Elizabeth went over to a chest of drawers and returned bearing a large hairbrush. The bristles looked mean and hard.

"Bend over."

"Oh please don't Elizabeth. I'll do anything you say."

"Bend over!" Sid felt Elizabeth push her over and she bent, feeling her bare bottom completely exposed.

"Ow!" she cried as the brush hit her hard on her bottom, "ow" again as the blows came quicker and faster, the bristles stinging sharply. The pain made her cry more at first, but then as she braced herself for each blow the crying lessened and she fell completely silent.

There was a pause and the blows stopped. Sid remained bent double, wondering if Elizabeth was just taking a rest.

"Stand up now."

Sid straightened up to face Elizabeth's eyes boring into her, still holding the hairbrush raised as if to strike her. Sid cowered.

"Well I hope that's taught you a lesson. If it hasn't I'll get my father to spank you when he comes home."

"I'll be good now, Elizabeth, really I will."

"We'll see, take off your pyjama top — quick!"

Sid struggled to pull it over her head and dropped it on the floor, the last shred of protection gone.

"Don't just throw your clothes on the floor like that. Hasn't your mother taught you better than that? Fold it and put it on your bed."

Sid obeyed. She moved across the room, feeling her nakedness a heavy weight of embarrassment and shame. She had never felt like that, naked with her mother.

"Go over to the window," said Elizabeth, turning out the light. She drew back the curtains and opened the window. It was dark now and there were no birds singing. No sound broke the quiet of the street.

Sid shivered and Elizabeth put her arm round Sid's shoulder. Sid flinched at the touch.

"See that house over there?" Elizabeth pointed across the street to the house directly opposite. Sid nodded.

"See the top bedroom window? There's a man lives in that room. He and I are friends. He's rigged up a pulley–line across the street from my window to his and we send each other messages. We use it to visit each other — at night."

Sid looked at the window opposite — it was dark. She tried to make out a rope strung across the street but couldn't see anything in the dim street light.

"He does things to me," continued Elizabeth, lingering on each word, "but you're too young to understand that. He does anything he wants to. If he knows you've been naughty, he'll whip you with his belt." She pushed Sid away from her.

"Stand in front of the window now and don't move. If you do, you know what'll happen. I'm going back to bed and I'll be watching you."

Sid stood in front of the window feeling the cold air attacking all of her body at once. She shivered. Wasn't this ever going to end? She'd thought that after the hairbrush she'd be allowed to go back to bed. Where was her mother? Was she never coming back? Was she going to be left in Elizabeth's charge for ever? She felt numb with cold and tiredness, though her bottom was still stinging. She shifted, crossing and rubbing her arms to try and keep warm.

"Stop fidgeting," came the voice from the bed.

"But it's cold here."

"Don't be silly. It's a warm night. Don't tell lies. If you fidget, he'll come over — and when I tell him what you've done, he'll start on you. You won't be very happy after that."

Sid tried to stay still, wondering what he was like and what he would do if he came. She remembered the two boys who had tied her to a stake when she was much younger, told her she was a witch and pulled a rope so tight that it burned her wrists and ankles, leaving bruises and red weals which didn't heal for days.

"He'll stick his thing in you," Elizabeth went on, "even if you are only a little girl — it'll hurt bad, worse than the belt. And then you'll be dirty, your father will hate you. No–one will ever want to marry you."

Sid wished her mother would come. She wasn't bothered about marriage. As long as her mum loved her still. But would she still love her after tonight? Would her mum think she was bad and dirty like Elizabeth did? She started to cry again.

"Stop crying or I'll spank you again!"

Sid wiped her nose with the back of her hand, disliking the slimy wet feeling. Then she saw a spotlight hovering on her stomach and moving down to her crotch where it came to rest.

"Did you like it when I touched you there?" asked Elizabeth, after what seemed a long silence, pointing the torch steadily at Sid.

"No," said Sid.

"Of course you did — liar. Tell the truth."

"All right then, I did," Sid tried again, willing this to be the right answer.

"You filth, what you've just said is dirty. I'll have to tell your mum. She won't half be shocked — and you only a little girl. She won't ever love you again."

"Oh please don't tell her," begged Sid. How did Elizabeth know what she had been thinking a few minutes before?

"What'll you give me for not telling?"

"Anything, I'll do anything — only please don't tell my mum. I've got some pocket money," she offered tentatively, after a brief silence.

"How much?"

"Half a crown." Sid saw herself standing in front of a counter full of sweets choosing what to spend it on — lemon sherbets or gob–stoppers? She forced the image from her mind.

"You can have it all," she said with only a tinge of regret in her voice.

"Big deal. It's not much."

"It's all I've got."

"Okay then. But that's not enough, you'll have to do something else for me."

"What?"

"You'll have to promise on your honour not to tell anyone about tonight. It's a little secret between us. If you so much as breathe a word to anyone, I shall know and then I shall tell your mum and my mum everything about you and you'd be for it. And I'll tell HIM to come and find you in the dark when you are all on your own..."

Sid remembered the terror she felt every night at home when her mother turned out the bedroom light and left her — the thuds and noises in the empty flat upstairs, the footsteps on the stairs, — the man, coming to get her. She saw him crossing endless ropes through the night to find her — oh yes he would find her.

"Cross your heart?"

"Cross my heart. Now can I get into bed?"

"In a minute, what's all the hurry?" Elizabeth ambled across the room and turned on the light. She stared at Sid and started giggling. "You don't half look stupid standing there starkers!" Sid thought she heard a good–natured tone in Elizabeth's voice, but she wasn't sure.

"Can I put my pyjamas on now?" She asked, wishing Elizabeth would turn the light off again so she wasn't so exposed.

"Just a minute — all in good time," said Elizabeth benevolently. "Now say after me: I am truly sorry for the dreadful way I've behaved tonight and for all the trouble I've caused Elizabeth."

Sid repeated the words falteringly.

"Say it again."

Sid obeyed, wondering if this was going to continue all night. Elizabeth suddenly tensed and moved nearer the door, listening intently.

"Can I put my pyjamas on — I'm cold!"

"Sssh, be quiet," hissed Elizabeth, listening a moment longer. "They're back now. Quick, get into your pyjamas and into bed. Hurry up!"

Sid ran to her pyjamas, pulled them on and leapt into bed, shivering with cold and relief. Apprehensively she watched Elizabeth come over to her bed and sit on it.

"Now," said Elizabeth," you've been very wicked but I've forgiven you so long as you keep your promise."

"Course I will," said Sid.

"That's good. Now you can have your goodnight kiss — then turn over and go to sleep."

Sid watched Elizabeth bend over and kiss her on the cheek. She turned towards the wall and shut her eyes. It was over. Her mum was back. She felt the lights go out and heard Elizabeth getting into bed. She waited awake for some time, hoping her mum would come in to kiss her. No one came. She heard steady breathing coming from Elizabeth's bed. Eventually, she drifted into a fitful sleep in which she dreamed she was standing by the window, watching him slide across a rope towards her.

***

Next morning Sid woke up and glanced anxiously over at Elizabeth's bed, relaxing when she saw she was still asleep. She raised herself and looked around the room. It had seemed so big the night before and now it looked so small.

The door opened and Elizabeth's mother came in to wake them. Elizabeth ignored Sid completely except to demand the half–crown she'd been promised. Sid took it out of her purse and obediently handed it over. Elizabeth took the purse and checked it was empty. Nothing more was said.

As Sid and her parents were leaving, Elizabeth's mother said to her: "Did you enjoy sharing Elizabeth's room with her?"

Sid felt Elizabeth staring hard at her. "Yes" she said.

"You must come again — on your own next time." A look of extreme anxiety crossed Sid's face, but she knew what she must say: "Thank you."

Elizabeth's manner was as polite as her mother's though a little colder. "Do come again," she said to Sid. "Bye!"

In the car, Sid's mother turned and asked her: "Did you have a nice time with Elizabeth?"

The events of the previous evening already seemed only half–real, like a weird and painful dream. How could she begin to explain what had happened? Her mum would think she was making up stories — so would anyone.

"Yes, it was alright."

Pauline Gooderson

NIGHT CREAMS

(for my mother)

A flat, cool sachet of face cream,
French, strong, sweet flower smell
For dry skin.
A night alone, with a book.
I wash and dry my face,
Before bed, early.

I rip the thin, smooth metal plastic
To cream my face.
I look in the mirror,
I see my mother.
I see her standing by her mirror
In her dressing gown,
With a pair of pants on her head,
Keeping the hair off her face.

She is vigorously cleaning her face
And rhythmically rubbing
Her night cream into the shapes
With firm, assured movements.
Quick, efficient, mechanical
With years of repetition.

Then the swift wringing of hands
As she rubs in her hand cream,
Perfunctory, not caressing.

I sob self–consciously
And move away from the mirror
Which speaks of her.
I want to be comforted.
I want her.

I cry knowing I can't be comforted,
And each time I wipe my eyes
I am overwhelmed by the scent
On my hands, her hands,
And the patterns of cleansing and creaming
I have learnt from her.

I felt closest to her then,
At that time of night.
I'd bring rehearsed teenage pleas
Into her bedroom with my goodnights.
"Can I go to the Arcadia on Saturday night?
I'm going with Moraig and her brother's bringing us home."
Or
"Can I stay at Moraig's this weekend?
I'll do my homework on Sunday night."

She seemed vulnerable and accessible
In her soft night–clothes.
And we both had one thing in common–
We were both getting ready for bed–
Her skin supple with French night–cream,
Mine lumpy with spots and Clearasil.

The evening dress I'd parade in that bedroom!
Ladybird jam–jams and Clark's slippers;
Long pink nightie with matching pink hairband;
Baby–doll frills with fluffy mule slip–ons;
Grandad shirt from Oxfam.
Now in my men's draw–string, stripey pyjamas,
I miss my mother.
Her smell, her firm lined hands,
Fingers fattened with arthritis.

I want to phone her.
It's a quarter to eleven,
She'll be in her routine now.
My father already in bed
In his sleeping position, head tucked,
Or reading a thick, library book
By the bedside light.
She doesn't read much
And can't get comfortable anymore
In bed.

How can I ring Ireland
Not sounding happy, gregarious, fulfilled?
Must never seem lonely or sad,
And certainly never cry.

But I phone. I weep.
"Mum?" Immediacy.
"What's wrong? Why are you crying?"
Anger and impatience frame her care.
I force laughter to reassure her
And say it's nothing. I am a coward.
"Are you alright?"
"Yes," I say boldly.
"I just missed you."
The bravest thing I've said all year.
"O for goodness sake!" she cries,
As if this matters little or not at all.
"I was just putting on some cream
And I thought of you with your knickers on your head!"
I'm really laughing now,
Embarrassed and close.
"Och, you silly old goat!"
She tuts and laughs.

Quickly she reasserts calm, social concern.
Her voice tightens.
"How's your work going?"
We chat, banal and comforting
For twenty minutes.
I ask her to phone me sometime
If she needs to, too.
"Yes Cherry." She says almost dismissively.

Her tone suggests that I'm going too far,
Showing too much.
"You're never in, anyway."
We laugh and say goodnight.

I go to bed early, alone,
Thinking of my mother.
Her skin, her night–creams,
My skin, her skin,
Falling against the pillow.

She sells sea–shells
On the sea shore.
Sea sells she–shells
On the she–shore...

Cherry Smyth

98

GRANDMOTHER

I see
Your sickly pink corsets
Unhooked in the evening
Hooked up again next day.

Your dresses — always blue
Your hairnets on the dressing–table
Live on ad infinitum

The smell of your flesh
A faint talcum–powdered sourness
Lingers in my nostrils.

You talk and shout in your sleep
You become another being
Frightened and fascinated
I listen.

Anne Hazel Clare

CARDIGANS

White is the summer colour,
Though hardly innocent.
White haired women,
White cardigans over patterned crimplene or cotton,
White shoes,
White handbags
Clamped firmly to their sides
By bent elbows.
British summer women
Marching firmly down the prom,
Into the church fête
Along the village street
In evening or Sunday best.

White armour holds thoughts at bay,
Of summers before the children left;
The cycle of years; endless chores;
Fighting to supply increasing needs.
Ashes of these struggles
Rest safe in the white bags
Between the battered photos and the pension book.

Jean Abbott

SHEROS

All my daughters are sheros
Heaven knows
Where they get it from — maternal
Grandmother, maybe,
A psychic, mystic sneaky old lady.

Each one she blessed
Youthful guests
At an old lady's deathbed.
Grandmother passing
Age old secrets to the young, laughing.

"Come, come, nearer, stand near..."
Small ear
Pressed close to old lady's whispering mouth.
Grandmother's bequest
To innocent, restless, puzzled guest.

My daughter sheros, older now,
Won't tell how
An old lady's breath sounded —
"Grandmother's secret!
Can't tell you today... tomorrow... maybe... not yet."

My daughter sheros rise up from table.
I am unable
To hold them back, tease out their secrets.
Grandmother's magic
Too subtle for a mother's trick.

So I'll wait my turn, daughter sheros,
Til who knows,
You bring me girl children, to my deathbed,
Grandmother's allies
Ready for blessing, young, old and wise.

Polly Thomas

I was your eyes
your arms your legs

I ran upstairs
for your glasses
I ran downstairs

upstairs, downstairs
in my lady's chamber
looking for her glasses

I always found them
when no–one else could

I'd return to your side
triumphant
bearing treasure —
the wounded glasses, one arm
strapped with tape,
the lenses dirty and clouded —

and you were pleased with me.

I helped you decorate
at your side
to pass a tool or hold a piece
of hanging sticky paper
threatening to envelop me
like a shroud
hating the wet glue
on my fingers in globs
but I must hold on,
mustn't let go —

you had to get it just right
I had to be just right
for you.

I cleaned the house
while you were out
I hoovered, swept, polished,
washed the bare boards
nails and splinters
stabbing my knees
hurrying on
wanting to surprise you —
one less chore for you —
but attentive to detail
knowing I must be thorough
do it exactly the way
you would do it —
nothing else would please you.

I wanted to save
your tired body
your ageing aching limbs
for better things
than housework —
my body was young
and didn't matter

I was a servant
not paid, not indentured,
trading my labour for your love.

Pauline Gooderson

TIME TRAVEL

I turn to Kath at the wheel. She's concentrating on the road, swinging the wheel round and back, changing gear. This is her first car, a second–hand Mini Metro. She passed her test a month ago and now we're driving home. I would have refused, but she offered to pay the petrol so I can't plead poverty, or British Rail, my only other excuse now I haven't a husband. I settle back and dream.

As a child, on treats, days out in the country in our ancient Ford Anglia, Mum would ask,

"What do the cows say?"

"I love Kathryn" she'd reply, without missing a beat. I'd sit in the back seat, a sour little goblin, who developed travel sickness and stopped the car.

Kath remembers that after Dad died, Mum traded his car to take us out. I remember that before he died, Dad refused to let her learn.

The radio snaps me back. We're on the motorway, cars zapping across the windscreen like a video game, changing lanes that make my stomach lurch, burning up the lads in the Ford Capri who whistle and yell. Kath drives her car cheap and loud like clothes from Top Shop, applying lipstick for police speed trap cameras, smoking out the window.

I feel dark and ugly, left behind. I want everything she has and nothing I have. Only she can do this, strip me of the years and my hard–learned politics, leave me desperate to belong to what I'd thought I'd left behind. But I always wear the wrong shade lipstick and embarrass her by being too clever or too loud. I'm possessed by the goblin self–pity. This is the mood I buy clothes I hate she never asks to borrow. This is the mood I get my hair chopped off and she says she liked it long. This is the mood I get married.

"Can we stop soon? For a coffee?"

"What for? We've only just got started. Light me fag, will yer?"

I'm the ultimate passenger. Trapped for the duration, up on the big wheel. You can see a lot from up here, but there's fuck all you can do about it.

"I love being driven" I'd said to Elliot, driving out to the Bar and Grill last Christmas. How I loved being fetched and carried, protected from the dark and journeys alone. How I loved the way he introduced me in his quiet, gentle voice. I slept with him for his car and married him for his social skills. No more standing on the edge with this perfect inter-mediary. Right? That was the time I wore my wedding ring and went out without keys or money. The cows loved Elliot too.

Kath's slowing for the services.

"You want a drink?"

"I'll get us some tea."

"Coffee for me, I'll phone Mum."

Kath has always been the messenger, the warm, affectionate one. My safety net, my home–not–home. A sister, but not a mother. Safer that way. We lived in the sound of the football ground. Saturdays were defined by its shouts. It seems Kath remembers the roar of triumph whilst I heard the silence of loss.

After Dad died, I remember Mum sitting on the stairs crying, a bunch of red bills in her hand. Kath held up her arms and hugged her. I held up my comb and said:

"Will you part my hair, please?"

Next time, I didn't make the same mistake. I was the one who made her laugh. I heard her in the kitchen, saying

"What would we do without her?"

Kath remembers the tears and the laughter whilst I remember the frantic search for words.

Now I spin stories in my head, feet dangling from the big wheel, clinging to my passenger status, driven and therefore not to blame.

Kathryn cried the day of my wedding. She didn't come. She wouldn't because I hadn't told Mum. In the end, six months later and one visit home when we slept in separate beds, I made Elliot tell her. They went off together for a walk. My Mum loved Elliot too.

Back in the car, Kath turns the window down and the music up.

"Drive carefully" Mum has said, but Kath has grown–up with her first car.

"Katy" says the goblin "is the one he cuddled when he got ill. The only time he played with his kids was when he was dying and you were too old to sit still by then. Men." Says the goblin sitting on my shoulder. "Can't live with 'em. Can't live without 'em."

"Piss off" I say.

I got dressed up on Christmas Eve and we drove to the bar. It was dark and there were lights on the porches and in the trees, reflecting off the snow. I could see my wedding ring glinting on the hand on his knee.

"Where to?"

"I'm in your hands" I said. "I love being driven. I'm the ultimate passenger."

And he laughed and looked over at me and didn't see the stoplight or the car and I pressed my feet on the floor and it swerved, honked, gestured asshole.

"Shit. You OK?"

"Fine."

But I look at him sideways and twist the ring on my finger.

We're going home. We're almost there. I want to misdirect her — the goblin whispers a short–cut round Glasgow, but she knows the roads like a homing pigeon and I can't get out now. I've never wanted to drive. I've always been scared of the power, the capacity to hurt and be hurt. I used to talk about being a trucker, but I was more interested in the long distance than the lorry– driving.

Back in London before we left, Elliot must have been packing up for law school when she called me.

"It's his last night, you've got to come. I'm taking him to the airport tomorrow. He said he was going to ask you."

"He would've called me."

"Come anyway. Same old place."

"I dunno."

"Don't be daft. I'll see you there."

Later that night, carrying a Sainsbury's bag of his old shirts, I turn up at the pub. Walking down the stairs, I'm slammed to a halt by the sight of Elliot with his arms around a woman I don't know, my sister behind and to the left, smiling up at me. The goblin swings into close–up on me and like Joan Collins, I'm left centre–stair, the title music stranding me till next week.

When I finally get moving again, I hand him the shirts and leave, all social skills deserting me, the goblin humming revenge in my head.

"Why did you do that?"

"Overtake that old biddy?"

"Why did you invite me to the pub if you knew he was with someone else?"

"I didn't know she'd be there."

"Why didn't you tell me he was seeing someone?"

"You got no right to be jealous."

"That's not the point. I shouldn't have been there. You made a fool of me."

"It's your own fault. He was so good to you, but you made him go. You just got to have everything. Look at your wedding, dressing in black. You just took the piss. You think you're clever. Well you're thick."

Kathryn, the blonde baby who lay in his lap, is the baby who cried so hard I thought her lips would snap. The truth is she doesn't remember anything, except a big, open mouth to which she now applies the brightest lipstick and the biggest smile.

"Kath, you remember that lad at the Roller Disco?"

"What about it?"

"And he told me he was going to chuck you?"

"And you never told me. You let me go up there."

"I said I couldn't protect you from pain. You had to learn."

"What a cow...What about it?"

"Nothing."

"This isn't going to be one of your stories is it?"

"Kath?"

"Yeah?"

"When we get back, will you teach me to drive?"

"No chance."

Janet Beck

105

DADDY, DADDY

Death makes people angry,
No–one likes being left.
My father died in Missouri
when I was four
and came back to life in California.
He told me his name was Puddin'tane,
but I knew it was really Lazarus.

Lazarus, living with Donald Duck
and Mickey Mouse in Redondo Beach.

Daddy, why?
What did I do wrong?
Was it because I didn't talk until I was two?
Was it because my hair wasn't blond?
my eyes weren't blue?

What's your name?
Puddin'tane. Ask me again,
and I'll tell you the same.

Dear Doctor Freud,
How does a little girl learn to love men
if her father exits early,
choosing death or some less gracious
form of departure?
Signed, WAITING TO KNOW.

Dear WAITING,
Don't worry.
Any man can be called Daddy,
it is actually only an alias.
I must add that there are some perversions
where men prefer to be called Puddin'tane.
It helps if you can remain flexible.

What's your name?
Puddin'tane. Ask me again,
and I'll tell you the same.

Daddy, are you truly dying?
I thought you were already dead.
How is it that you never look any older?
In every ageing photograph,
You are always a young Clark Gable —
and I am forever four.

Mary Jo Bang

FAMILY SNAPSHOT

It always seems to be at this point that his smell suddenly lunges out from him; knocking us all sick with fear on the familiar waves of it. So potent we can almost see it, surging out from under his skin and slamming against the doors, the windows. Thump! So the room thickens and dies with his stench and we seven are stuck suddenly in syrup air. Daddy–flavoured.

And this is the point where his gritty thumbs begin to unwind from the rims of his jeans pockets. Where his fingers drum towards his waist as if looking for some imaginary typewriter on which he can tap out the lists and lists of our sins. Tacker tacker. But this is where they grasp instead, the cold heavy buckle of his belt. This is where, with no fumbling and no need to look, he flicks it quickly open.

And we are as glued to his movements as if we are hypnotised. But pride tugs hard and makes us pull away our gazes, to run them quickly wild in search of some other thing (anything) of fascination.

And there above his head, a deep yellow strip of sticky fly- paper spirals gently from the ceiling; licking out at live flies. Today's catch is still buzzing. A high staccato buzz. Still beating thin, fragile wings with enough force to make the paper spin. But with legs so stuck it will never fly anywhere again.

And we listen. Listen intently as our fly tells us its story of long glory-days, yellow with sunshine, suddenly eclipsed. Noticing all the while from the corners of our eyes, dad's thick hairy–knuckled hands as they begin the slow pull on his belt. And here the buzzes shorten dramatically to a warning tone. ZZ. ZZ. Watch out. Reminding us of light–bulb sockets which frazzle little children into over–toasted strips. ZZ. It could be as quick as that.

But no. This time, in the dangerously increasing silences, the belt–snake is sliding slowly, vertebrae by vertebrae, past the denim loops. It slinks upwards, charmed by the dance of the dying fly; rising slow, slow, slow. Very, very high. It's head gripped till it must choke, by his huge meatball fist. We swallow and we know...no–one is going to stop this.

And now a high whimper hiccups behind us as it is suppressed. We know it is our mum. Pleading past us with her eyes. And him ignoring her, although tomorrow he will try and please her until she forgives him. Until she loosens her tongue and speaks to him again. But right now... well... nothing's going to stop him now.

And which one? Which one? Our fly is silent forever now. The snake's tail hanging free and momentarily limp while a scrabble of panic lets loose in our minds. Who's it to be? Who will be first? Which one? The snake whirrs suddenly through the air. Whoosh. Crack! It smacks its lashing tongue against the ground, taking in the feel of it. Warm–up exercises. But it is enough to rend the air. To forge a gap where, at last, our high voices can scream through. "No Dad." "No." "Please no!"

And mum takes the chance to talk. Quiet. Trying a new tack.

"Bill man, take it easy. They're only tiny," she reminds him.

So we soften our faces as much as possible, trying to live up to her words. Surely he can see we are not much more than babies?

But the snake is taken and doubled till it's buckle–head bites it's own rounded tail and it's belly sags in a loop. It is a noose swinging loose but ready to grab and jerk tight. It is a mouth open in a large 'O' of surprise. A mouth too shocked to even cry.

And this is a familiar point again. Where he leaves the belt doubled for extra weight. For extra pain. Where he begins to make weary commands. This is tiring him, his tone says. This is so exhausting. It is hurting him more than it will hurt us.

"Bend over."

And this is where we look around at each other slowly, oh so slowly, as if trying to ascertain exactly which one of us he is talking to. Slowly, slowly — knowing it is irritating him right through, so the lash will sting all the more when it finally falls against our skins. But we play for time. Something might happen in those extra few seconds. That same god which had allowed the fly to die might look down on us and take more pity. A neighbour might suddenly be given the notion how her throat is so dry and tight that nothing will help it better than the exercise of a long, half–way–in–the–door chat and the soothing balm of our mum's tea.

But no salvation knock comes to our door as he indicates the arm of the settee. One by one we are to bend over there. And later we will cry all night and mum will sneak upstairs to see us and rub germolene into our bodies while we suck in air sharply at her touch.

And this is where he begins his terrifying procession of names. And where he chooses Colin first. Where Colin rebels as instantly as we all know he will. He shakes his head. No. No. No. Walking backwards from dad's advances. No. Screaming strange choking sounds. His mouth and eyes wide open, but his throat narrowing against the rising fear and screams. He chokes and coughs until he sounds like he is dry retching. Mum pleads "Bi–i–ill!" And now that the child is cringing in a ball in the corner, wet with tears and spewed spittle, he allows himself to back off. All the while promising Colin that he will still get his turn later. That he can now wait till last. And after he has waited all that terrible time he will be given twice as much as anyone else, for his obstinacy.

And this is where Colin is reduced to something we daren't look at. We begin to cry for him. Quiet tears, because we daren't make a sound for fear of bringing attention to ourselves. Quiet tears, hoping dad will some-how forget what he was planning to do. Hoping he will have to stop and try to remember.

And, meanwhile, that Saviour neighbour with the dry throat could be getting closer and closer. She could almost be at the door by now... surely.

Sheila Cragg

Mother
the long arm of death
reaches towards you
slowly

You turn to me
fear runs
helter–skelter
down the wrinkles and lines
of your face
your eyes shrieking pain
you turn to me

Mother, I can cradle you
like a child
stroke your hair and face
kiss a moment's rose
back into your cheeks

But I cannot stand between you and death
cannot negotiate better terms
on your behalf

This time I can only look on
a powerless spectator
feel only my own pain
at the thought of your leaving.

Pauline Gooderson

THE COFFEE TABLE

I don't know why we called it a coffee table, no–one drank coffee and though, admittedly, it was a table, we treated it with such off–handedness, it could have been a cardboard box for all we cared.

The important thing was; it was there. My father hated it and habitually demonstrated his loathing by heavily plonking his feet on it whenever he was home.

When the folks were out Billy used to hold illicit card games — the table's surface strewn with cigarettes (legal and illegal), beer cans, cards, money and bits of paper noting I.O.U.'s.

Sundays, without fail, Mummy would polish every inch of it with an obsessive love she reserved only for inanimate objects. The more father defiled it, the more Mummy would wax and shine it and honour it with gifts; vases of flowers, stiff, abrupt crochet'd doilies and small brightly coloured glass animals.

On weekday afternoons, Mummy and the table played host to a constant stream of friends.

That's when she really came alive, like a hungry cat on the verge of obtaining its next meal, her ears sharpened to the living–room tattle, her eyes darted quickly from speaker to speaker and at the slightest request she would spring up overly eager to please.

"A piece more of yuh grata cake, luv."

"Beg yuh bring some sugah sista B."

But by evening she had retracted to that inaccessible silence we all understood and, in a way, demanded.

That morning I had been staring out of the upstairs window surveying the road with growing apprehension. She'd already been gone three weeks and unlike all the times before we were beginning to take her seriously.

Each evening since she'd been gone, father would work himself into a frenzy of self–pity.

"I don't know what wrong with that woman, everything yuh know, everything she want I give her and every damn time I turn roun' vroops! she gone."

Me and Billy acted like we didn't care.

Eventually Pastor Morris arrived with his van. He was his usual jovial self.

"Alright darling, you looking well handsome today — still giving the boys hell eh?"

He and Billy quickly loaded the van, being careful to check the list Mummy had sent; a few clothes, the hair dryer, a couple of pairs of shoes, towels and so–on.

Father stood in the doorway scrutinising every item while Pastor Morris cracked jokes and prattled away continuously.

He said he'd only come for a few things.

He said Mummy was staying with Aunt Ethel for a couple of days.
He said he was sure things would work out, we weren't to worry, she'd be back in no time.
Father slammed the door on Pastor's cheerios and the three of us gathered together in the living room, staring at the four, smooth, deep, round wells in the carpet.
 We knew, this time, she'd gone for good.

a–dziko Simba

SOME KIND OF DESPERATION

There were three groups at dinner that evening in the small, brand–new hotel at Marmaris, Turkey. A couple in their late thirties and a family of four, both arrived that evening, and the largest group of eight who'd already been there for a week or so.

These eight were English tourists, ranging in age from twenty to sixty. When the other families were in bed and trying to sleep, and the hotel owner and his family were praying for rest, the group of eight tourists were just livening up. The hotel owner was eager to please, eager to establish his enterprise, but oh, so tired.

It was one a.m. with no sign of a let up. He'd been on his feet since six a.m. and would have to rise at that hour again this very morning. His wife was exhausted. It had pained him to see his children drawn through the long hours, so he'd sent them all to bed and tried to cope alone.

Haw haw haw haw haw. These people were like stupid mules. What could they find to laugh at so much? They didn't really seem happy. The desperation of their laughter told him so. And it was some kind of desperation that drove them in this manner through the night. They hung on hungrily for one of their party to make a half–joke so they could explode into laughter. Someone else would say a thing that seemed slightly amusing and they'd burst out again with that strange harsh laughter. They'd drink and throw their heads back and scrape their chairs and think in their drunkenness what a good time they were having. For they felt very isolated here. They saw what they lacked and couldn't face it, because their lives were empty — no richness, no warmth, no power nor passion, no fabric, no feeling, no pride. They were floating on the debris of their lives and clinging to a peculiar formality, with no thought for others – because in this desperate struggle for life, another person's lack of a few hours sleep was unimportant.

They sang, they cheered, they clapped each other and shouted their laughter and each one inside had sunk beneath his sadness.

The family of four, one only a toddler, tossed and turned in their beds. Angry and resentful and tired. They were Turkish. They wanted to relax. They wanted to enjoy their family and their time. They'd travelled all day, eaten their meal and retired at ten. Ahead lay five hours of the baying of human laughter 'till at last, at three a.m., all had quietened down but bleary–eyed and tense, sleep had escaped them — save the two–year old who slept like an angel sprinkled in sweat.

The couple in an adjacent room lay side by side — he asleep, she awake with those so open eyes. So open eyes that told on her so thoroughly.

At dinner that evening, the two–year old had toddled amongst the diners, in and out of chairs being the cutest nuisance. The couple had eaten despondently and were now nursing their coffees. He was Turkish, she was English and they were in their late thirties. He was attentive but there didn't seem to be anything of lovers about them. They were on

113

holiday but there was nothing of holiday–making about them. She seemed tired and sad. She watched the little boy as if transfixed. Her husband was looking elsewhere, lost in his thoughts and apart from his wife as if they were strangers either side of a screen.

She watched the boy with an intensity of hope and wilting love, faded but clinging to a wilting body. The most primal of love was all that was left of this woman. It had consumed her in its battle for its own way. There was nothing left but the need. No more thought or logic or understanding or appeasement. No compromise or resolve or adjustment. And in this hot land of hot blood and hot desire, she knew the flame of her womanness would burn bright — its brightness for this, the last time. There was only death of a thousand kinds beyond and a death fighting for the power of her womb.

So now they lay side by side, two of a spent species, having performed the ritual of their love–making. A holiday had been recommended. She herself had heard of people who'd gone away to enjoy themselves and completely forgotten their long plan for a family — and had conceived. But she hadn't forgotten, or given up. She wasn't enjoying herself. Perhaps she would — later. This was the first exhausting day. And she was too exhausted to plan enjoyment.

She was a peculiar woman, always swathed in clothes — anorak, thick cardigan, dress, neckscarf — as if wrapped up from the sun, not wanting a drop of its golden rays to touch her skin. At first, one might suppose she was following Turkish custom to dress in layers, but it was just her way. Underneath all the clothes she was a painfully thin woman; skin taut against bones that jutted out gangling and awkward. Her neck was long and scrawny, her hair tussled, frizzed, mid–length, mid–brown, shapeless. Her eyes glared out her pain from red sockets. The shadows beneath adding ten years to her looks. Her skin pale, her lips thin from too many years of drawing them in against fate.

On her second day of this holiday, she went for a long trek in the hills, alone with her husband. The scenery was breath–taking, but it was hard to remain amazed at scenery for more than one day and she hadn't. She wasn't accustomed to much walking so the expedition was exhausting, and something in her made her despise her kind husband's efforts at creating romance for them. She was bloody tired and there was a sharp wind the whole day long, pushing and pushing into her back. At last they returned to the hotel. She flopped into bed and fell into an exhausted sleep.

The next day she couldn't move from backache and her husband went out alone. It seemed the fates were mocking her with her silly little holi-day–to–conceive. She had such little strength left to get her to her goal. And she resented dissipating it in polite spurts of joviality.

The day after, their fourth, they went to the busy street market, full of cheap wares and good utility items and clothes. It was enjoyable but she tired so easily these days. She said nothing — for she kept most of her feelings even from her husband and continued traipsing round. At last

114

they came again to their starting–point, but her husband began the circuit again.

She felt so utterly done in. Not physically. It was seeing so many mothers with their children. Each laugh, each word between them was a sharp pain to her — 'till, a wounded pin–cushion of a woman, she simply stopped. The shutters came down. She was lost in her own world and her husband, just by looking at her, knew that all thoughts of niceties were beyond her.

They went and sat by the marina's edge. He talked at length of a boat trip the next day, eventually going back across the road to book their tickets. He was a very long time. She sat in the sun waiting for him. Watching the families walk by. Seeing them look at her and knowing what they saw. And knowing, quite clearly this time, that it was the end. It was as sudden as that. The mothers walking by were too young, too pretty. The sun had already taken out the month–old colourant from her hair and looking in the mirror that morning, she was shocked to see how grey she'd become. The sunlight too was cruel. It illuminated every wrinkle and for the first time she couldn't think of herself as young–ish anymore. She was bordering middle age. She was no longer attractive now youth had gone. Youth that gives the plainest of people a certain beauty, slips away unnoticed from our mirrors.

Such were the thoughts that ran through her mind. And she had nothing left. Not a morsel of energy. She was past it. Long past, if only she'd known, conceiving a child. Yes, women in their forties had babies but they were sturdy, zestful souls, resoundingly fit and healthy. She'd never have a child. She knew that as surely as she knew there'd be no life for her without one. It was crystal clear and she was tired beyond endurance.

But the weariness had plateaued into some kind of peace. A certain calm. Yes. The air was balmy. People floated to and fro. Everything was as nothing. It was the end of the road. The boats bobbed dreamily before her, moored lazily in file and tightly lined up. In the distance children came out of school and laughed delightedly amongst themselves and no–one noticed the drab–looking woman who silently slipped between the boats and beneath the water.

She felt the hot tears of her eyes for the last time as the cold water of the sea washed over them and claimed them for her own.

Ayshe Raif

115

GOING HOME

Mother–Land
Land of the Mother
Mother of the Land

    your daughter in exile
    who'd rather be that
    than Alien at Home

        is coming back
        is coming back
        is coming back

red roses in hand for the treasures that were and might not be
weapons lying low for the treasures that were and might not be
mourning black for the shackles that were, are and will long be

Nina Rapi

THE MAGIC CARPET

Half drunk at night
I sit on the living–room floor
Eyes down on the carpet
Axminster Persian

Swirls of fuzzy arabesque
Hypnotise me.
Interlacing scrolls
Transport me
To bazaars
Where men in turbans
Cross–legged
Haggle over prices...
To shady tea gardens
Where intellectuals
Chin in hand
Haggle over ideas.

I am back in Istanbul
Grey minarets
Sober
In blue blazing skies.

"Allah is great!" wails the afernoon prayer.
I wander in the shade of giant plane trees
Past a cat family licking avid lips
Outside the butcher's.

A shadow pattern of plane leaves
Dances on the sun–cracked pavement
While down a glaring concrete hill
Lies the deep azure of the sea
The sea always returning the mind to itself
Stretches out to the islands
Hazy pyramids steeped in blue vapour.

The city alien yet intimate
Struggles to exert its influence.
Streets uneven and haphazard
Alert the individual
A wrong step here
A broken ankle there.

Inside your house now
On the Golden Horn
Warm heavy air
Struggles sluggishly
Through shuttered windows
Hardly refreshing perspiring foreheads.
A plate of water melon
Icy from the fridge
Stands tempting on a copper table.
Your mother is offering us her favourite fruit.

You sit behind your newspaper
Clinging to affairs home and foreign
The smoke from your cigarette unfurls to the ceiling.
I observe the downward curve of your lips
And lay my hand on your blue denim thigh
I murmur your name...

A voice in my ear booms
"Want a drink? Hey, wake up!
Penny for them! Hey!
You're back there again, aren't you?
And she's there with you."

Back
In Clapham now
My eyes are on the carpet
Axminster Persian.
They are full of tears.

Anne Hazel Clare

THE GREEN GLASS BOTTLES

I was a guinea–pig.

My school days in the suburbs of Sydney, Australia took on new meaning when my father told me, years later, that my school there had been taking part in a State–run educational experiment.

Feed on demand. Or, give the children as much knowledge as they want. I enjoyed it, not knowing it was happening. I became greedy for new facts and figures about the world, an addict for calculating longitudes and latitudes, a book–worm who exhausted the school library's stock of books. I won prizes, became class captain. Excelled.

The school was large. Trawling children from the surrounding new estates, it numbered over seven hundred pupils. The upper and lower schools were laid out opposite each other but identical. Light, low–level buildings around a bitumened playground used for holding open–air assemblies.

Orange dust and cracked earth in summer, a hint of grass in winter, the playing–fields were trampled daily in the chase for footballs, volleyballs, softballs, basketballs. Sport was the symbol of new Australian endeavour. It raised us up as a people, our ancestry in scattered continents paled, as we beat back the primitive bush around the nation's edges and competed internationally.

Sports day was the climax of all this fervour. Dressed in our green and gold kit we were bussed to the ground where rival schools would battle it out for supremacy. The day began with the ritual march round the ground. Each team had been drilled, eyes dead ahead, limbs operating like the parts of a human machine, we moved forward, the school banner leading.

Once, our rhythmic pounding of the turf so impressed the judges, they declared us winners. Victorious in our ability to submerge our individual selves in one single moving mass, we felt a pride in our belonging.

Within the school there were honours of a different kind. In the library, two large varnished wooden boards dominated. On the left, one which recorded the names of the school's brightest and on the right another inscribed the names of those elected to be Head of School. The names and the dates were carved into the wood and immortalised in gold. Divinity, or very nearly.

Imagine... what if? It would be a first for the school. Dux and Head Girl. I stared and stared at the boards imagining the letters there already. My name enshrined... twice.

My parents had other ideas. They were dreaming of old, cold, distant England and a different life. They sold the house and booked our passage on the ocean liner. They tried to win me over with tales of exotic Tahiti and Acapulco cliff–divers. And the Panama Canal, what a miracle of engineering, that was, wasn't it? I wasn't fooled. I kept seeing the varnished boards in the library and my name up there in gold.

119

My idea of England was a freezing, foggy place where people with cockney accents lived in rows of grim little houses, like I'd seen on 'Coronation Street'. I was convinced there couldn't be a scrap of countryside left that wasn't built on. How did they fit all those people into such a tiny space? My parents laughed. They were going home.

The school bell rang out. It was an oppressively hot day and I was loathe to leave the darkness on the shady side of the school to run the bleached out square of the softball pitch. The bell rang again and I felt a sharp pain as I jumped down the steps onto the hot black bitumen. There was a gash, deep and red in my skin. A friend passing, stopped and started crying. It came to me slowly that my body bled, that the sticky redness flowing onto the bitumen was mine. A teacher came and stood at the top of the steps surveying the scene. My friend calmed down. I looked accusingly at a sharp iron bracket sticking out from the wall, meant for a wooden seat, but only half–finished. The workmen had gone, complaining of the heat. It was over a hundred degrees. Too hot to work, to think, to feel any pain. Or, perhaps it was the shock.

The teacher carried me to his new Ford family car and lay me on the back seat. When he lifted me out again at the local clinic I stared back at the blood staining the immaculate upholstery. Unable to contact my parents they debated whether to give me an anaesthetic. I watched as they sewed the wound in my leg together, stitch by stitch until it was finished. The red flow staunched.

I gave my parents the blue report card. Inside a fraction which read one over seven hundred and fifty. They said nothing, only closed it and packed it in a box full of others like it. When the school voted me Head Girl I mumbled apologetically and felt like a traitor. After all, I was leaving them for England, the land of the Poms.

England. Snow in April. Bought an overcoat. My first. Chilled to the bone, I kissed the cheeks of ageing relatives whose names became a blur, whose hands pressed chocolates and fifty pence pieces into mine. At first, we stayed with my grandfather and his young wife. His fourth.

The house looked sad and naked. Elms which had once graced the front had been replaced by a concrete drive. Here and there were traces of the original house, the home of a Southern Squire. But now the wind howled and crept inside at every juncture. Of the forty rooms, mostly empty, we lived in half a dozen. There were windows everywhere uncurtained, looking onto the Solent waters. They drew my gaze to every passing tanker, tub and dinghy. I used to shut my eyes tight at the sight of an ocean liner. But the wish remained even so and I saw myself stowed away in the bowels, heading out to sea for reunion with the wide brown land of my birth.

Grammar School seemed meaningless. My Australian vowels, mocked, were soon replaced by a kind of standard English I borrowed from the television. Village life meandered, turning on nuances of division I found absurd. Unwilling and unable to understand my place within the British class system I spent years testing boundaries and confounding expectations of the kind of girl I ought to be.

***

Fifteen years later, married and pregnant I returned to Oz. We had to forgo the Singapore stopover and fly straight to Sydney. Thirty–two hours and a lifetime later I was back on homeground.

I swam in the warm blue sea, lay on the smile of a wide, white sandy beach. Went walking in the rainforest and smelled eucalyptus gum burnt on a fire. I introduced my husband to the taste of tea boiled in a blackened billy can.

To outsiders, we were pommy tourists going snorkelling on the coral reef and sailing round the coral islands. We hired a car and travelled thousands of miles along narrow, rutted highways, crossing dried–up river-beds, passing mile upon mile of white–barked gums. Then sudden out-breaks of bush fires with flames leaping across the road and the sickening smell of dead kangaroos rotting on the roadside, victims of Australia's new civilisation. I saw my country now as I had never seen it and knew I was asking if this was the place to let my unborn child see life.

Of course, I took my husband to visit my old school. We sat in the hired car and watched the children run out of the school gates laughing and joking. I touched the smooth skin on my leg. The two inch scar was burning.

I wouldn't go inside though. Wouldn't go into the library. This is what I'd come for. My curiosity to read the names in gold on the boards. Which of my forgotten classmates had found their way onto those plaques? But I sat in the car, frozen. Feeling a rage grow within me, that they were rewarded. That their lives grew on, uninterrupted. That they were never dragged kicking and screaming on board a ship. And I was back there, clinging to the railings and staring through salt tears as the coastline was slowly reduced to a sliver, out past the 'Heads' of the harbour into the wide ocean beyond.

Heading back to the North Shore on an ancient ferry, the harbour looked inviting with it's majestic blue reflecting back the creamy shells of the Sydney Opera House. The distant 'Heads' seemed only a memory now that I was back safe inside the harbour's embrace. When we passed Pinchgut, a prison island I'd visited as a child, the texture of the thick stone walls came back to me and I touched again, the iron rings they used, to chain down convicts with dreams of escape. How many had risked the swim from the island to the shore–line and made it?

My own dreams came flooding back. Dreams of diving overboard from the luxury floating prison which had transported me from the colony of my birth, back to the old world of my parents. Dreams of escape as we tramped northward across the Pacific and plans I'd hatched, standing for hours at the stern of the ship, searching the foamy wake of my child's life for a clue.

121

There had been a ceremony as we crossed the equator. A man dressed as Neptune was thrown into the pool. I'd marked the day in my own way, by throwing a green airtight bottle into the sea with a scribbled pencil message inside. I'd watched it for as long as I could, screwing up my eyes until finally, it had bobbed out of sight.

***

Our holiday over, cases packed, we drove from Narraweena to the airport with my paternal grandmother talking persuasively of the advantages to pensioners of living in the suburbs of Sydney, rather than eking out an existence somewhere on the South Coast of England.

Soon we were flying back to Perth, across the enormous wastelands of middle Australia, where we would stop briefly before leaving the continent en route for Bombay. High over the darkness of the Pacific Ocean, I dozed off during the in–flight movie and dreamed I saw my green glass bottle floating in the bay of a palm–covered island...

'A fisherman, trawling in his net picked out the rusty–topped green bottle and saved it for the skinny brown boy who always greeted him on the beach. The boy collected every kind of old bottle. He cleaned them and polished them and filled them with delicious roast nuts. On a make–shift stall at the end of the beach, he haggled with tourists over a few centimes, to get the best price for each one of his treasures...'

Behind me in the 'plane, the small Italian boy who'd been kicking the back of my seat on and off from Sydney, managed to give me one more jolt as he rolled over in his sleep. I gave up trying to follow the convolutions of the movie plot, stretched out across the entire row of three seats and fell into an uneasy sleep. When I awoke we'd already crossed the equator. There was no ceremony, not even a token mention from the captain and for some reason I felt sad to have come so far without any sense of the distance.

In Bombay and Dubai, we wandered like lost souls for hours in the deserted airport lounges, waiting for the plane to be cleaned out and refilled with fuel, water, and inedible food. Europe beckoned with every tedious, sweaty moment we spent sitting and musing on tea and toast, cool air and fresh clothes, hot baths and clean sheets.

The next day, we glided effortlessly onto the runway at Heathrow and looked out on a grey English morning.

"Glad to be back?" my husband asked.

"Soon be home now", I replied, as we passed each other coats to keep the cold from our newly–suntanned bodies.

Cheryl Robson

THE PARADISE GARDEN

In the paradise garden
We sit.
Watching peach stain purple
In the darkening sky
And oil tankers glide guilelessly
Across the sea.

Among the silhouettes of cypress trees
Black against purple
The fairy lights flick on.

A waiter passes.
You summon him
Polite but peremptory.
Your mouth is not a rosebud
No.
It is a thin curving line
With a tendency to droop
A cigarette holder of a mouth.
You order paradise cocktails
A speciality of the house.

Dusk falls.

Your brightly flowered blouse
Is fading into shades of grey.
A spark flies up
From your American cigarette
Glows and dies.
And now you are silhouetted with the cypress trees
Black against purple.

Night grows
And blots you out.
Only your eternal Marlboro
Sends up signals to the moon.
I sit clueless and untuned —
A vague jumble of wave lengths
Drifting from one thought to the next.

And now
resuscitated by the evening lull
Dead sounds come to life —
The melancholy hoots of ships
Emancipated from the daytime roar,
Steel tips of heels
Clanking on concrete,
Cars purring down the cobbled hill outside,
Ice clinking in glasses,
Lovers' mumbles from other tables
And your voice asking for the bill.

Anne Hazel Clare

WALKING OUT OF THE BURNING HOUSE

Walking out of the burning house,
calmly, slowly,
into a soundless night;
a pillow under one arm,
a book in my hand,
chosen at random.
Sharp points of cold gravel
pressing into the bottom of my bare feet.
Soles too soft,
like worn flannel.
The sky glowing like a hot ember.

Then I remember —
too late —
the photographs.
A man in plaid shirts
two boys always dressed alike,
a young woman in yellow silk.
The images blacken, melt,
and disappear.

I keep walking along a straight path
across a green lawn
which leads toward something unseen.
Never looking back;
the house full of flames;
and no regret.

This is the dream.

Mary Jo Bang

IN SICKNESS

Argos Orestiko, small cobbled streets
thick flokates and fear of meningitis

age twelve walking alone
always alone yellow–skinned, scraggy, ugly
and cursed with brains, damn you
Be plump, a little dumb and
scrub your skin white, now that's a girl
head bent, hands in pockets
schizophrenia is a knife
between me and the world
and so much more that
i must cut out
        the mad spinster, the one i must find out about
        she keeps her house locked up
        her windows all nailed shut. she wants to see
        no–one. she won't even let the sun in.

        they say she's gone off her troubled head
        off to some strange place, was too smart,
        asking too many questions. Do you hear that?
        Don't you do that now!

Nina Rapi

THE ALTERNATIVE

Friendless in playground corners
Silent on the edge of conversations
Violent in fights and confrontations
She stands accusing and accused.

Naughty girl
Not interested in sewing and knitting
She longs for the knotted branches
Of trees
The mysterious undergrowth
Of neglected gardens.

She throws away her dolls
And refuses to pray for forgiveness.
She says no to confirmation
An atheist by the age of twelve.

A thousand adult tongues tut tut their disapproval
A thousand adult eyebrows are raised over cups of tea.

Naughty girl
Not interested in babies and cooking
She talks to herself in French
Smokes cigarettes out of bedroom windows.
The future is an open sky.

Not knowing what she's going to do
Not knowing where she's going to go
She dreams of tangled forest floors
Where roots and tendrils
Intertwine.

Anne Hazel Clare

RESOURCE DIRECTORY

compiled by Jean Abbott

It became apparent while researching this section that information on all types of writing groups is very patchy. Women involved in running groups would be well advised to inform the Literature and/or Drama Officer of their Regional Arts Association of their existence, as well as any other arts organisations in the area.

Libraries usually keep lists of all local groups. The information can be mutually beneficial as they can pass on details of courses, grants and other initiatives as well as telling interested newcomers about your group. It is also likely that local women's centres or local council women's units will know of women only groups in their area. Phone numbers for many women's centres are listed in the Spare Rib Diary. Information on playwriting workshops, courses, competitions and grants may be obtained from:

The New Playwrights Trust
Whitechapel Library
77 Whitechapel High Street
London E1 7QX.
071 377 5429

and from the Regional Arts Associations. Standard reference books available in most public libraries include :

"The Writers and Artists Yearbook" (A & C Black)
"The British Theatre Directory" (John Offord.)
"The British Alternative Theatre Directory." (Conway McGilliray)
"Contacts" (Spotlight)

Annually updated lists of many types of women's groups may be found in the Spare Rib Diary. A Directory of Writers' Circles throughout the country may be obtained from :
Jill Dick, Oldacre, Horderns Park Road, Chapel–en–le–Frith, Derbyshire SK12 6SY.
(Current price £3, but most groups listed are mixed.)

The Arts Council Poetry Library in the Festival Hall carries details of many writing groups, events and competitions. 071 921 0943/0664

Short women only courses are organised by:
The Hen House
Haverby Hall, North Thoresby, Lincs. DN36 5QL 0472 840278
and mixed courses, often led by women by:
The Arvon Foundation
Lumb Bank, Hebden Bridge, W. Yorkshire, HX7 6DF. 0422 843714
and at Totleigh Barton, Sheepwash, Beaworthy, Devon EX21 5NS. 040923
338

* Indicates groups which organise occasional courses and workshops
rather than meeting on a regular basis.

London and South–East

Women's Writing Workshops
Aphra Video
The Diorama, Peto Place, London NW1. 071 485 2105
Asian Women Writers' Workshop
30 Wesley House, 4 Wild Court, London WC2 5AU. 081 806 5824
Preethi Manuel 081 291 4116
Centerprise
136 Kingsland High St. London E8 2NS. 081 254 9632.
Clean Break Theatre Company (Women with prison experience)
c/o Wesley Hse, 4 Wild Ct. London WC2. Alexandra Ford 071 405 0765
Commonwealth Institute Women Writers' Workshop
High St. Kensington, London W8. 071 603 4535
East London Work Collective Women's Writing Group
(081 945 8720/071 249 5180)
Hoxton Hall Women's Writing Group
130 Hoxton St. London N1 071 739 5431
Irish Women's Writing Network
c/o Aine Collins, Oxford House, Derbyshire St. London E2
Munirah Theatre Company (African women)
91 St Ann's Rd, London N15 6NU. 081 809 6985.
Northwest Women Writers
c/o The Stables, Dollis Hill Lane NW2. 081 452 1685.
Outcast
(Gay and Lesbian Group) 071 267 1419.
Paines' Plough: The Writers' Company *
123 Tottenham Ct. Rd. London WC1 071 380 1188
Resisters' Theatre Company
11 Mowll St, London SW9. 071 582 6643.

Second Wave Young Writers
Albany Empire, Douglas Way, Deptford SE8. Annie Considine 081 691 8016.
The Soho Poly Theatre (The Soho Group) *
16 Ridinghouse St, London W1. 071 636 9050
The Women's Playhouse Trust*
Garden Studios, Betterton St. WC2. 071 379 0344
The Women's Theatre Group*
5 Leonard St. London EC2A 4AQ. 071 251 0202.
The Women Writers' Workshop
c/o The Drill Hall Arts Centre, 16 Chenies St. WC1. 071 631 1353.
Kent
Julie Rainey, 66 Canterbury Road, Whitstable, Kent CT5 4HD
Berks.
Moving On Women's Community Theatre
Penny Henrion, 31 College Road, Reading, Berks 0734 505106
Surrey
The Network of Women Writers Association
8 The Broadway, Woking, Surrey GU21 5AP

Bookshops
Books Plus
23 Lewisham Way, London SE14 6PP 081 691 2833
Compendium Bookshop
234 Camden High St. London NW1 071 485 8944
Gay's the Word Bookshop
66 Marchmont St. London WC1 081 969 7654
Silvermoon Women's Bookshop
68 Charing Cross Road, London WC2H 0BB 071 836 7906
Sisterwrite Bookshop/Craftshop and Gallery
190 Upper St. London N1 071 226 9782
Women and Children First
16 The Market, Greenwich London SE10 9HZ 081 853 1296

Film and Video
Albany Video
Albany Empire, Douglas Way, Deptford. SE8 081 692 0231
Aphra Video
The Diorama, 14 Peto Place, London NW1 4LH 071 935 5365
CEDDO (Training courses prioritising Black Women)
South Tottenham Education and Training Centre
Braemar Road, London N15 5EU 081 802 9034

Cinema of Women
31 Clerkenwell Close, London EC1R0AT 071 251 4978/7
Cinestra Pictures
The Co–op Centre, 11 Mowll St. Lo ndon SW9 6GB 071 793 0157
Circles Women's Film and Video Distribution Ltd.
113 Roman Road, London E2 0HU 081 981 6828
Irish Women's Video Production Group
London Irish Women's Centre
59 Stoke Newington Church St. London N16 071 249 7318
Pictures of Women Ltd.
10 The Pavement, Clapham Common, London SW4 071 249 9632
Women in Sync
Units 5 & 6, 47–51 Wharfdale Road, London N1. 071 278 2215
Women's Radio Group
90 de Beauvoir Road, London N1 4EN 071 241 3729

Midlands and East Anglia

Women's Writing Workshops
Cambs.
Better Half Women's Theatre Co–operative
Contact Liz Goodman 0223 353388
Staffs
Distaff
Isabel Gillard, St Lawrence Cottage, Sellman St. Gnosall, Staffs.
ST20 0EP
Beds.
Flitwick Women Writers
Jean Abbott 0525 712606
Milton Keynes Women's Writing Group
Anne Mason 0908 321274
Norwich
Norwich Women's Centre, 53 Melrose Road, Norwich NR4 7PN
0603 628130
Notts.
Trellis Women's Writing Network
Sue Thomas 0602 231896
Birmingham
Young Women's Writing Group
Annette Field, Flat 4, 401 Gillott Road, Edgbaston, Birmingham
B16 9LL

Women in Theatre
Friends' Institute, 220 Moseley Rd, Highgate, Birmingham.
021 440 4203.

Bookshops
Cactus Community Books
2b Hope St, Hanley, Stoke–on–Trent, Staffs. ST1 5BS.
Common Ground Co–op
190–192 Alum Rock Rd, Saltley, Birmingham.
Grapevine Books
Unit 6, Dales Brewery, Gwydir St, Cambridge. CB1 2LJ.
The Ikon Gallery
58–72 John Bright St, Birmingham B1 1BN.
Key Books
136 Digbeth, Birmingham B5 6DR 021 643 8081
Mushroom Books
10–12 Heathcote St, Nottingham. NG1 3AA.
Phoenix Books
93 Warwick St, Leamington Spa, CV3 4RJ.
Wedge Co–op,
13 High St, Coventry, West Midlands. CV1 5RE.

Film and Video
Cinewomen – Norwich Women's Film Weekend
c/o Cinema City, St. Andrew's St. Norwich NR2 4AD 0603 622047
Vokani Film Circuit
Unit 40, Devonshire House, High St. Digbeth, Birmingham B12 0LP
021 773 4260
Second Sight Video Workshop
Zair Works, 111 Bishop St. Birmingham B6 6JL 021 622 5750

Wales and West Country

Women's Writing Workshops
South–West
Ann Sponnoble, 17 Trevethan Rise, Falmouth, Cornwall. TR11 2DX.
South–West Women's Arts Network
Caroline Purslow/Josie Sutcliffe
Salem Chapel, Broadhempston, Totnes, Devon TQ9 6BD 0803 813293
Women's Creative Writing Group
Pat West, 69 Lower Redland Road, Bristol BS6 6SP
Wordwomen
c/o Bristol Broadsides 0272 240764

Wales
The Magdalena Project
Chapter Arts Centre, Market Rd, Canton, Cardiff. CF5 1QE.
Made in Wales Theatre Company*
Mt. Stuart Hse, Mt. Stuart Sq, Cardiff. CF1 6EL.
Bookshops
Arnolfini
16 Narrow Quay, Bristol, Avon. BS1 4QA.
Bilbo's Books
New Bond St. Buildings, Bath, Avon. BA1 1BE
Harvest Wholefoods
37 Walcot St, Bath, Avon.
Theatre Clwyd
Yr Wyddgrug, Clwyd. CH7 1YA.
In Other Words
72 Mutley Plain, Plymouth. PL4 6LF.

North

Women's Writing Workshops
Bridge Women Writers' Group
c/o Bridge Project, Sulgrave Hall, Manor Road, Washington,
Tyne and Wear.
Chorlton Women Writers
WEA Class, contact Ailsa Cox 061 227 9344
Fringe Ltd. Community Arts Training Organisation
Jan McVerry/Erica Rushton, 63 – 67 Tithebarn St. Liverpool.
Kenton Women Writers' Group
W. Coghill, Kenton Library, Hailwood Avenue, Kenton,
Newcastle–Upon–Tyne.NE6 5DY
Liverpool Women Writers' Group
c/o Shirley Jones, 74 Lark Lane, Liverpool L17.
Merseyside Women's Anthology Group
c/o Anne Cunningham, Catalyst, Methodist Centre, Beaconsfield St.
Liverpool. L8 2UP.
Nailah Black Women Writers' Workshop
Victoria McKenzie, 24 Althonsus St. Old Trafford, Manchester
M16 7QS. 061 226 5000
The Next Stage Northern Women Writing for Theatre
Christa van Raalte c/o 38 Sydney Grove, Wallsend, Tyne and Wear
NE28 9HD 091 263 0466
North East Playwrights
Jan Maloney/Julia Darling, 29A Claremont Place,
Newcastle Upon Tyne. NE22 4AA. 091 221 247

Northern Gay Writers
Liz Rutherford, Commonword, 21 Newton St. Manchester M1 1FZ.
061 236 2773
North West Playwrights' Workshops *
Melanie Harris, Contact Theatre, Oxford Road, Manchester M15 6JA
061 274 4418
Women's History, Women's Lives Group
c/o Eileen Kelly, Second Chance to Learn, Room 9, City College,
Clarence St. Liverpool, L3 5TP.
Womanswrite
Liz Rutherford, Commonword, 21 Newton St. Manchester M1 1FZ
061 236 2773
Writing Women
10 Mistletoe Rd. Newcastle–Upon–Tyne, NE2 2DX

Bookshops
Alleycat Books Co–op
28B Sutton St, Durham.
Beano Wholefoods
36 New Briggate, Leeds LS1.
Editions Ltd.
Bluecoat Chambers, School Lane, Liverpool, L1 3BX.
Grassroots Books
1 Newton St. Piccadilly, Manchester M1 1HW O61 848 9783/2
Independent Bookshop
69 Surrey St. Sheffield S1 2LH 0742 737722
News from Anywhere
112 Bold St. Liverpool L1 4HY 051 708 7270
Page One
9 Princes Ave, Hull, N. Humberside. HU5 3RX.
Single Step Co–op
78A Penny St, Lancaster, Lancs, LA1 1RJ.

Film and Video
Vera Productions
30–38 Dock St. Leeds LS10 1JF 0532 428646
Sheffield Film Co–op
Brown St, Sheffield, S1 2BS. 0742 727170
Women's Independent Cinema House
90–92 Whitechapel, Liverpool, L1 6EN. 051 709 3087

Scotland

Women's Writing Workshops
Edinburgh Playwright's Workshop*
Traverse Theatre, 112 West Bow, Edinburgh, EH1 2PD.
Glasgow Feminist Writers' Group
day: 041 942 7922/eve: 041 945 3032
New Playwriting Scotland Newsletter*
Royal Lyceum Theatre, Grindlay St, Edinburgh, EH3 9AX.
031 229 7404.
Women–in–Profile*
Kate Henderson, 5 Dalhousie Lane, Garnethill, Glasgow G3.
041 334 3333

Bookshops
Boomtown Books
167 King St, Aberdeen, Grampian, AB1 1TJ.
West & Wilde Bookshop
25A Dundas St. Edinburgh EH3 6QQ 031 556 0079
Stirling University Bookshop
The McRobert Centre, Stirling, Central, FK9 4LF.

Ireland

Write for information about writing workshops to:
Theatre Ireland Magazine
67 Donegall Pass, Belfast, BT7 1RD.
Fred Hanna Ltd. Belfast Civic Arts Centre*
Old Museum Arts Centre, Belfast*
Abbey Theatre*
26 Lower Abbey St, Dublin 1.

Bookshops
Attic Press Books
44 East St, Dublin 2.
Books Upstairs
36 College Green, Dublin 2.

Bookworm Community Bookshop
16 Bishop St, Derry, N. Ireland. BT48 6PW.
Quay Co–op
24 Sullivan Way, Cork.

Women's Centre Shop
27 Temple Lane, Dublin 2. 0001 710088

Related Organisations

British Theatre Association
Cranbourne Mansions, Cranbourne St, WC2H 7AG. 071 734 1664
Cambridge Women's Resources Centre
Hooper St. Cambridge CB1 2NZ 0223 321148
Feminist Archive
Trinity Road Library, St. Phillips, Bristol BS2 0NW. 0272 350025
Feminist Book Fortnight
c/o 7 Loddon House, Church St. London NW8 8PX 071 402 8159
Feminist Library
5 Westminster Bridge Road, London SE1. 071 928 7789
Lesbian Archive and Information Centre
BCM 70005, London WC1N 3XX. 071 405 6475
The Pankhurst Centre
60–62 Nelson St, Chorlton–on–Medlock, Manchester, M13 9WP.
061 273 5673
Society of Authors
84 Drayton Gardens, London SW10 9SB. 071 373 6642
Theatre Writers' Union
c/o The Actors Centre, 4 Chenies Street, London WC1E 7EP
071 631 3619
Women in Education
The National Association, PO Box 149, Preston, Lancs. PR2 1HF
Women's Education Project
129 University St. Belfast BT7 1HP 0232 320212
Women in Publishing
Gillian Armstrong c/o Butterworths, 88 Kingsway, London WC2.
071 405 6900
The Writers' Guild of Great Britain(Women's Committee)
430 Edgware Road, London W2 1EH. 071 723 8074

Women's Publishing Houses

Attic Press
44 East Street, Dublin 2 0001 716367
Battle Axe Books
Kim Werts 071 603 1139
Black Women Talk
PO Box 32, 190 Upper Street, London N1 071 354 3186

Honno Welsh Women's Press
Ailsa Craig, Heol Y Cawl, Dinas Powys, De Morgannwg CF6 4AH
Karia Press
628 Tottenham High Road, London N17 081 801 4375
Madlove Publishers
PO Box 61, Northants NN1 4DD
Only Women Press
38 Mount Pleasant, London WC1X 0AP 071 837 0596
Pandora Press
15–17 Broadwick St. London W1V 15P 071 439 3126
Sheba Feminist Publishers
10a Bradbury St. London N16 8JN 01 254 1590
Stramullion Publishers
11A Forth St. Edinburgh EH1 3LE 031 556 0246
Virago Press
Centro House, 20–23 Mandela St. Camden Town, London NW1 0HQ
071 383 5150
Women's Community Press
144 East Essex St. Dublin 2, Eire 0001 712149
The Women's Press
34 Great Sutton St. London EC1V 0DX 071 251 3007
Womenwrite Press
P.O. Box 77, Cardiff CF2 4XX 022 496062
Zed Books Ltd.
57 Caledonian Road, London N1 9BU 071 837 4014

Publications

Everywoman
34 Islington Green, London N1 8DU 071 359 5496/7
Feminist Arts News
105 Gladstone St. Bedford MK41 7RS 0234 219966
Feminist Review
11 Carleton Gardens, Brecknock Road, London N15 5AQ
International Women's Resource Centre
173 Archway Road, London N6 081 341 4403
Lesbian and Gay Socialist Quarterly
PO Box 83, Southall, Middlesex. UB1 1QR
Manchester Women's Liberation Newsletter
Grass Roots Books, 1 Newton St. Manchester M1 1HW
Pink Paper
42 Colebrook Road, London N1 8AF 071 226 8905

Shocking Pink II
23 Tunstall road, London SW9 071 274 0412
Spare Rib
27 Clerkenwell Close, London EC1R 0AT 071 253 9792
Tears in the Fence
Hod View, Stourpain, Blandford, Dorset 0803 867625
Trouble and Strife
Women's Centre, 34 Exchange St. Norwich, Norfolk
Women's News
185 Donegall St. Belfast BT1 2FJ 0232 222823

Grants, Awards and Bursaries.

Eileen Anderson/Central Television Drama Award.
Central Television, Central House, Broad St, Birmingham.
Arvon Foundation International Poetry Competition.
Kilnhurst, Kilnhurst Lane, Todmorden, Lancs OL14 6AX.
Arts Council of Great Britain Writers' Bursaries.
105 Piccadilly, London W1V 0AU.
Authors' Club First Novel Award.
The Authors' Club, 40 Dover Street, London W1X 3RB
Verity Bargate Award
The Soho Poly Theatre Club, 16 Ridinghouse Street,
London W1P 7PB
Alice Hunt Bartlett Award
The Poetry Society, 21 Earls Court Square, London SW5
H.E Bates Short Story Competition.
Leisure & Recreation Dept. Northampton Borough Council,
Guildhall, Northampton.
Samuel Beckett Award.
Faber & Faber, 3 Queen Square, London WC1N 3AU
Bridport Arts Centre Creative Writing Competition
Arts Centre, South Street, Bridport, Dorset.
Bristol Old Vic & HTV West Playwriting Award.
Playwriting Award, PO Box 60, Bristol BS99
Commonwealth Writers' Prize.
Book Trust Publicity Office, 45 East Hill, Wandsworth,
London SW18 2QZ
Rose Mary Crawshay Prize
The British Academy, 20 – 21 Cornwall Terrace, London NW1 4QP
The George Devine Award
23 Ainger Road, London NW3.

Eastern Arts Writing Fellowship
University of East Anglia, University Plain, Norwich. NR4 7TJ.
Fawcett Society Book Prize.
46 Harleyford Road, London SE11 5AY
Greenwich Festival Poetry Competition.
25 Woolwich New Road, London SE18 6EU.
The Guardian Fiction Prize.
The Guardian, 119 Farringdon Road, London EC1R 3ER.
**E.C. Gregory Trust/The Francis Head Awards/Tom Gallon Trust/
Travelling Scholarships**
The Society of Authors, 84 Drayton Gardens, London SW10 9SB.
Irish Bursaries in Literature.
The Arts Council, 70 Merrion Sq. Dublin 2, Ireland.
London Newspaper Group Short Story Competition.
London Newspaper Group, Newspaper House, Winslow Road, London
W6.
LWT Plays on Stage.
LWT Plays on Stage, South Bank Television Centre, London SE1 9LT.
**The Mobil Playwriting Competition for the Royal Exchange
Theatre Company.**
Royal Exchange Theatre, St Ann's Square, Manchester M2 7DH.
National Poetry Competition.
The Poetry Society, 21 Earls Court Square, London SW5 9DE.
Northern Arts Literary Fellowship and Writers' Awards
10 Osbourne Tce, Jesmond, Newcastle upon Tyne. NE2 1NZ.
Catherine Pakenham Award
Evening Standard, 118 Fleet Street, London EC4P 4JT.
Radio Times Drama/Comedy Awards.
BBC Publications, PO Box 1AX, 33 MaryleboneHigh St. London W1.
The Royal Literary Fund.
144 Temple Chambers, Temple Avenue, London EC4Y ODT.
Ryman New Writers' Award.
Sinclair Prize for Fiction.
Book Trust, Book House, 45 East Hill, London SW18 2QZ.
PO Box 38, Chelsea, London SW3 3NL.
W.H. Smith Literary Award./W.H.Smith Young Writers' Comp.
W.H. Smith, 7 Holbein Place, London SW1W 8NR.
Southern Arts Literature Prize and Bursaries.
Southern Arts, 19 Southgate Street, Winchester, Hants SO23 9DQ.
Thames Television Playwright Scheme
Thames Television House, 306–316 Euston Rd, London NW1 3BB.
West Midlands Arts Creative Writing Attachment
Brunswick Tce, Stafford. ST16 1BZ.

Welsh Arts Council Prizes.
Welsh Arts Council, Museum Place, Cardiff, CF1 3NX.
Whitbread Book of the Year/Whitbread Literary Awards.
The Booksellers Association of Great Britain & Ireland,
154 Buckingham Palace Road, London SW1W 9TZ
Yorkshire Arts Association Literary Awards.
Glyde House, Glydegate, Bradford, BD5 OBQ.
Young Observer Teenage Fiction Prize.
Young Observer, Chelsea Bridge House, Queenstown Rd, London SW8.
Young Writer Awards (Spectator & Sunday Telegraph).
The Spectator, 56 Doughty Street, London WC1 2ll.

BIBLIOGRAPHY

On Writers and Writing

AUERBACH, Nina *Communities of Women: An idea in Fiction.* (Harvard Uni. Press 1978.)

BARKER, Howard *Arguments for a theatre* (Calder)

B.B.C. *Writing for the B.B.C.* (B.B.C. Publications 1974.)

Best Radio Plays (Methuen/B.B.C.from 1978)

BELL, P. Roseanne *Sturdy Black Bridges: Visions of Black Women in American Literature.* (Anchor Books 1979.)

BENNETT, Rodney *The Writer's Approach to the TV/Film script.* (Harrap 1976.)

BETTELHEIM, Bruno *The Uses of Enchantment.* (Peregrine 1978.)

BRANDE, Dorothea *Becoming a Writer* (Macmillan Paperback)

BRANDT, George *British Television Drama.* (Camb.Uni.Press 1981.)

BRICKMAN, MACDONALD & STARK, *Corrupt Relations: Dickens, Thackeray, Trollope, Collins and the Victorian Sex System* (Colombia Uni. Press 1978)

BROWNSTEIN, Rachel *Becoming a Heroine: Reading about Women in Novels.* (Penguin 1984)

CALDER, Jenni, *Women and Marriage in Victorian Fiction* (Thames and Hudson 1976.)

CHAMBERLAIN, Mary ed. *Writing Lives; Conversations between Women Writers.* (Virago 1988.)

CHRISTIAN, Barbara *Black Women Novelists: The Development of a tradition.* (Greenwood Press 1980.)

DAMES, DIVA and GRIMES, Janet *Towards a Feminist Tradition; An annotated bibliography of novels in English by Women from 1891– 1920.* (Garland 1982.)

DAVIDSON, Cathy N. and BRONER E.M. eds. *Mothers and Daughters in Literature.* (Frederick Ungar 1980.)

DELANY, Sheila *Writing Women: Women Writers and Women in Literature, Medieval to Modern.* (Shocken Books 1984.)

DUNBAR, Janet *Scriptwriting for television* (Museum Press 1965.)

FADERMAN, Lillian *Surpassing the Love of Men: Romantic Friendship and Love Between Women from the Renaissance to the Present.* (The Women's Press 1985.)

GILBERT, Sandra and GUBAR, Susan *The Madwoman in the Attic: The Woman Writer and the Nineteenth Century Literary Imagination.* (Yale Uni. Press 1979) *No Man's Land; The Place of the Woman Writer in the twentieth Century. Vol 1. The War of the Worlds.* (Yale Uni. Press 1989.)

GOREAU, Angeline *Reconstructing Aphra; a social biography of Aphra Benn* (The Dial Press 1980)

GOULIANOS, Joan ed. *By Woman Writt; Literature from six Centuries by and about women.* (New English Library 1973.)

GOOCH, Steve *Writing a Play* (A & C Black.1989)

HEILBRUN Carolyn G.and HIGONNET Margaret eds. *The Representation of Women in Fiction* (John Hopkins Uni. Press 1982.)

HUF, Linda, *A Portrait of the Artist as a Young Woman: The Writer as Heroine in American Literature* (Frederick Ungar 1983)

HYEM, Jill *Entering the Arena: Writing for Television.* 'Boxed In; Women and Television.' ed. Baehr, Helen and Dyer, Gillian.

JELLICOE, Anne *Community Plays.* (Methuen.)

KAPLAN, Janet, Sydney *Feminist Consciousness in the British Novel* (Uni. of Ilinois Press 1975.)

KELLEY, Mary *Private Women, Public Stage.* (Oxford Uni. Press 1984.)

MARKS, Elaine and de COURTIVRON, Isabelle eds. *New French Feminisms; An Anthology.* (Harvester Press 1981.)

MILLER, Beth ed. *Women in Hispanic Literature; Icons and Fallen Idols.* (Uni. California Press 1983.)

MILLET, Kate *Sexual Politics* (Virago 1977.)

MOERS, Ellen *Literary Women* (The Women's Press 1978.)

NEWTON, Judith Lowder *Women, Power and Subversion. Social Strategies in British Fiction.* (Methuen 1985)

POLTI, Georges *The Thirty–six Dramatic Situations.* (The Writer Inc.1989.)

RICH, Adrienne *On Lies, Secrets and Silence.* (Virago 1980.)

RUSS, Joanna *How to suppress Women's Writing* (The Women's Press)

SAUTTER, Carl *How to sell your screenplay.* (New Chapter 1988)

SELLARS, Susan ed. *Delighting the Heart* (The Women's Press.)

SHOWALTER, Elaine *A Literature of their Own: British Women Novelists from Bronte to Lessing.* (Virago 1978.) *The New Feminist Criticism.* (Virago 1985.)

STUBBS, Patricia *Women and Fiction: Feminism and the Novel, 1880 to 1920.* (Methuen 1981.)

SWAIN, Dwight V. *Film Scriptwriting* (Focal Press 1976.)

TATE, Claudia ed. *Black Women Writers at Work.*

TAYLOR, Cecil P. *Making a t.v. play* (Oriel Press 1970.)

TODD, Janet M. *Women's Friendship in Literature.* (Columbia Uni. Press. 1980.) *A Woolstonecraft Anthology* (Polity 1989.)

WALKER, Alice *In Search of Our Mother's Gardens.* (The Women's Press 1984.)
WANDOR, Michelene *Look Back in Gender. Sexuality and the Family in Post-war British Drama.* (Methuen 1987.)
WATTS, Emily Stipes *The Poetry of American Women from 1632 to 1945.* (Uni. of Texas 1977.)
WOOLF, Virginia *A Room of One's Own, A Writer's Diary* (Grafton Books 1977.)

General Interest;

BAKEWELL, Joan & GARNHAM Nicholas *The New Priesthood.* (Penguin 1970.)
de BEAUVOIR, Simone *The Second Sex.* (Penguin 1972.)
BERNARD, Jessie *The Future of Marriage.* (World Publishing 1972.)
BERNHEIMER, Charles and KAHANE, Claire eds. *In Dora's Case: Freud, Hysteria, Feminism.* (Virago 1985.)
BRUNT, Rosalind and ROWAN, Caroline *Feminism, Culture and Politics.* (Lawrence and Wishart 1982.)
CHERNIN, Kim *The Hungry Self.* (Times Books 1985.)
CHESLER, Phyllis *Women and Madness* (Allen Lane 1974.)
CHODOROW, Nancy *The Reproduction of Mothering.* (Uni. California Press 1978.)
DALY, Mary *Beyond God the Father: Toward a Philosophy of Women's Liberation* (Beacon Press 1973.)
DAVIS, Angela *Women, Race and Class* (1981)
DEUTSCH, Helene *The Psychology of Women.* (Grune & Stratton 1944.)
DICKSON Anne *The Mirror Within.* (Quartet Books 1985.)
DOWLING Colette, *Perfect Women* (Fontana 1989.)
DWORKIN, Andrea *Letters from a War Zone* (Secker and Warburg. 1988)
EICHENBAUM, Louise and ORBACH, Susie eds. *Understanding Women* (Basic Books 1983.) *Outside In, Inside Out.*
ERNST, Sheila and GOODISON Lucy eds. *In Our Own Hands.* (The Women's Press.)
FRANTZ Fanon, *Black Skin, White Masks.* (Grove Press 1967.)
FRIDAY, Nancy *My Mother Myself.* (Fontana 1979.)
FRIEDAN, Betty *The Feminine Mystique* (Penguin 1963.)
GAVRON, Hannah *The Captive Wife.* (Pelican 1965.)
GREER, Germaine *The Female Eunuch* (McGibbon & Kee 1971.)
GRIFFIN, Susan *Woman and Nature : The Roaring inside her* (The Women's Press.1984.) *Pornography and Silence* (The Women's Press 1981.)
HODGSON John & RICHARDS Ernest *Improvisation* (Methuen 1966.)
JANEWAY, Elizabeth *The Powers of the Weak.* (Alfred Knopf 1980.)
JOHNSON, Keith *Impro* (Methuen 1981.)

KITZINGER, Sheila *A Woman's Experience of Sex* (Penguin 1985.)
KRZOWSKI Sue and LAND Pat eds. *In Our Own Experience* (The Women's Press 1988.)
LAING, R.D. *The Politics of the Family* (Vintage Books 1972) *The Divided Self* (Penguin 1960.)
MEAD, Margaret *Male and Female* (Penguin 1971.)
MILLER, Alice *The Drama of the Gifted Child* (Basic Books 1981) *Thou Shalt not be Aware.* (Pluto 1984.)
MILLER, Jean Baker *Toward a new Psychology of Women* (Penguin 1978.)
MITCHELL, Juliet *Woman's Estate.* (Penguin 1971.) *Psychoanalysis and Feminism.* (Macmillan 1982.)
OAKLEY, Ann *Sex, Gender and Society.* (Temple Smith 1972.) *Housewife.* (Penguin 1976.)
PAYNE, Karen ed. *Between Ourselves; letters between mothers and daughters.* (Picador 1985.)
PIZZEY, Erin *Scream Quietly or the Neighbors will hear* (Hillside N.J. 1977)
RACK, Philip *Race, Culture, and Mental Disorder* (Tavistock Publications 1982.)
RICH, Adrienne *Of Woman Born: Motherhood as experience and Institution.* (Virago 1977.)
ROWBOTHAM, Sheila *Women's Consciousness, Man's World.* (Penguin 1973.) *Hidden from History* (Penguin 1975.)
SHARPE, Sue *Just Like A Girl* (Pelican 1976.)
SICHTERMANN, Barbara *Femininity; The politics of the personal* (Polity Press 1986.)
SPENDER, Dale *Invisible Women: The Schooling Scandal* (Writers and Readers 1982.) *Man Made Language.* (Routledge & Kegan Paul 1980.)
SPOLIN, Viola *Improvisation for the Theatre* (NW Uni. Press 1983.)
WOOLSTONECRAFT, Mary *A Vindication of the Rights of Woman* (Penguin 1978.)

Selected Poetry & Short Stories;

ADCOCK, Fleur ed. *20th Century Women's Poetry* (Faber 1987)
ASIAN WOMEN WRITERS WORKSHOP *Right of Way* (The Women's Press 1988)
BURFORD, Barbara ed. *Walking the Tightrope: New Love Poems by Women.* (The Women's Press 1987)
BURNETT, J. COTTERILL, J. KENNERLEY, A. NATHAN, P. eds. *The Common Thread: Writings by Working Class women* (Mandarin 1987)
CARTER, Angela ed. *Wayward Girls and Wicked Women* (Virago 1986.) *Black Venus* (Picador 1986.) *The Bloody Chamber* (1979)

CHOPIN Kate *The Awakening and other stories*. (Penguin)
COBHAM Rhonda & COLLINS, Merle eds. *Watchers and Seekers: Writing by Black Women in Britian*. (The Women's Press.)
CONLON, Faith ed. *The Things that Divide us* (Sheba 1988.)
Holding Out by North–West Women Writers (Crocus Books, Cheetwood Hse, Manchester.)
COSMAN, Carol ed. *The Penguin Book of Women Poets*. (1978.)
COUZYN, Jeni ed. *The Bloodaxe Book of Contemporary Women Poets: Eleven British Writers*. (Bloodaxe 1985.)
FELL, Alison ed. *Seven Deadly Sins* (The Serpent's Tail 1989.)
MCLEOD, Marion & WEVERS Linda eds. *One Whale singing & other stories*. by New Zealand women writers. (The Women's Press.)
OSLER, Audrey *Speaking Out; Black girls in Britain*. (The Women's Press.)
PARK, Christine & HEATON Caroline eds. *Close Company* (Virago 1987.)
LIVIA, Anna & MOHIN, Lilian *The Pied Piper: lesbian feminist fiction* (Onlywoman 1989)
McEWAN, Christian *Naming The Waves: Contemporary Lesbian Poetry* (Virago 1988)
THE RAVING BEAUTIES *In the Pink. No Holds Barred* (The Women's Press 1983 & 1985.)
ROWE, Marsha ed. *Sex & The City* (Serpent's Tail 1989.)
SCOTT, Diana *Bread and Roses; Women's Poetry of the Nineteenth and Twentieth Century*. (Virago 1982.)
SHEBA COLLECTIVE eds. *Serious Pleasure* (Sheba 1989)
SWANSEA, Charleen & CAMPBELL Barbara eds. *Love stories by new women*. (The Women's Press.)
WALKER, Alice *You can't keep a good woman down* (The Women's Press.)
WASHINGTON, Mary Helen ed. *Stories by Contemporary Black Women Writers* (Virago)
Wildish Things. by Irish Women Writers (Attic Press 1989.)

Selected Plays;

BEHN, Aphra, *The Rover, The Lucky Chance* (Methuen/RSC)
CHURCHILL, Caryl *Plays 1, Serious Money* (Methuen)
DANIELS, Sarah *Neaptide, The Devil's Gateway* (Methuen/RC)
DAVIS, Jill ed. Lesbian Plays (Methuen Theatrescripts 1987)
DEVLIN, Anne *Ourselves Alone* (Faber)
GEMS, Pam *Piaf, Camille*. (Penguin)
HYEM, Jill *Equal Terms* (Samuel French) *Post–Mortems* (New Playwright's Network) *Remember Me* in *Best Radio Plays 1979.*

JELLICOE, Anne *The Knack, Sport of my mad mother* (Faber)
LAVERY, Bryony *Origin of The Species* Vol. 6 *Plays by Women*. (Methen)
LEVY, Deborah *Heresies, Eva and Moses*. (Methuen.)
MCINTYRE, Clare *My Heart's a Suitcase* (Nick Hern.)
PAGE, Louise *Tissue, Salonika and others* (Methuen.)
RAIF, Ayshe *Caving In*. (Methuen) *Cafe Society* (Samuel French)
RAME, Franco *Female Parts*. (Pluto)
WERTENBAKER, Timberlake *Our Country's Good*. (Methuen/RC.)
WYMARK, Olwyn *The Gymnasium and others, Best friends and others*. (Calder.)
WANDOR, Michelene ed. *Plays by Women* Vols. 1 to 6 (Methuen.)
Dead Proud Plays by Young Women (The Women's Press.)